STRING BEAN, BUSTER, THE GRUMPY GOURMET AND OTHER PERSONAS: A MEMOIR

Philip M. Coons

iUniverse LLC
Bloomington

STRING BEAN, BUSTER, THE GRUMPY GOURMET AND OTHER PERSONAS: A MEMOIR

iUniverse books may be ordered through booksellers or by contacting:

iUniverse LLC
1663 Liberty Drive
Bloomington, IN 47403
www.iuniverse.com
1-800-Authors (1-800-288-4677)

ISBN: 978-1-4917-2322-7 (sc)
ISBN: 978-1-4917-2323-4 (e)

Printed in the United States of America.

iUniverse rev. date: 01/29/2014

"In the course of twenty crowded years one parts with many illusions. I did not wish to lose the early ones. Some memories are realities, and are better than anything that can ever happen to one again."
Willa Cather, *My Antonia*

CONTENTS

DEDICATION

Dedicated to my niece, Caroline, who loves to
hear family stories about her father and me

ACKNOWLEDGMENTS

There are a number of people to whom I owe a strong debt of gratitude. I am deeply grateful to my wife, Liz, who patiently listened to my memoirs as I read them as after-dinner entertainment. She laughed at all of the appropriate places and offered kind words of encouragement as I labored to complete this volume. She also acted as my editor, often as we drove together on short trips and vacations.

I also want to thank Karen Zach, former Montgomery County, Indiana Historian. It was Karen who initially interested me and encouraged me in my story-telling endeavors.

My interest in writing a memoir was piqued by Arthur Sterne, Ph.D., whose own memoir, *Things I Know or Think I Know or Thought I Knew or Who Knows?*, is a *tour de force*. Art has been a member of a memoir group at All Souls Unitarian Church in Indianapolis for over twelve years and it has been one of his favorite life experiences.

After hearing about Art's unique and gratifying experience I wanted to join a memoir group of my own, but none was available. Then my wife joined a memoir group at our church, but sadly it was only open to women. So I patiently waited.

In early 2013 a memoir group started at the Mid-North Shepherd's Center in Indianapolis. Entitled, "I've a Story to Tell," this group is ably led by Carolyn Lausch, a retired English teacher. Initially I was the only male member and a number of members were a good deal older than I. Only two of the women were my contemporaries. Finally Bernard joined and I was no longer the only male. All of the group's members are superb writers, so I consider myself extremely lucky to be in such good company.

INTRODUCTION

Memoirs have been around a long time, but during the late twentieth century memoir writing came into its own, so much so that the memoir genre has suffered and has been much maligned and criticized. There are memoirs of Hollywood personas, usually ghost-written. There are memoirs written by those with various mental illnesses such as schizophrenia and bipolar disorder. I've read numerous, often badly written memoirs, by authors with multiple personality (now known as dissociative identity disorder or DID), usually documenting therapeutic misadventures of the worst kind. Some of these are coauthored by the former DID author's naive therapist. Of course, there are memoirs written by people without serious mental illnesses who survived childhoods filled with the most horrible and tawdry kinds of abuse imaginable. If memoirs were movie genre, these might qualify as action-adventure films.

My favorite memoirs are usually written by folks with advanced degrees in English. These folks can write. Curiously, most well-written memoirs usually include something about the person's spirituality.

My memoir is none of these, so it's unlikely to be a best-seller and possibly will be of greatest interest to my family and close friends. This memoir is filled with stories or little memoirs about significant episodes in my life, some happy, some sad, and some humorous. It recounts the highlights and summarizes precious memories from my almost seventy years.

I have organized my memoir chronologically where possible, so the first seven chapters extend from my first memories through my career as a psychiatrist. The remaining chapters cover my hobbies, family, spirituality, and other momentous events in my life.

Most people mentioned in this memoir are mentioned by first name only. In some cases first names have been changed and in some instances a few facts have been changed or omitted to respect an individual's privacy.

Although I have attempted to fact-check a few items, as in all memoirs, these are my memories. Other people involved in my memoirs may have different recollections of the same events. But, that is alright. We all have selective recall, shaped by our viewpoints, especially when events happened so long ago.

So to you who chose to read this memoir, happy reading. Please enjoy and begin writing your own memoir.

CHAPTER 1

THE EARLY YEARS

"At about age four I can remember getting my mouth washed
out with soap in the kitchen for using 'bathroom talk.'"

IN THE WOMB AND SHORTLY THEREAFTER: MY PARENTS' REFLECTIONS

The following are excerpts from my book, *Letters Home from a WWII "Black Panther Artilleryman"* (Bloomington, Indiana: iUniverse, 2012), which is an edited collections of my father's letters to mother and my mother's letters to Clara, her mother-in-law, while Dad was serving during WWII.

My Mother

"I don't know where you're reading this, but hold on and prepare for a shock. Yes, I am gaining weight, 4 pounds already, but I'm also bulging at the seams of my clothes for I'm about 3 1/2 months pregnant! I was going to wait until the folks came in February to tell you and them but they didn't think they can come now and I need my maternity slip and nighty I left in Columbus, so I thought I'd better be telling. I hope it won't worry you any, because I feel just grand and have all along. I didn't have nausea at all. I guess I'm lucky at that. Harold knew too, before he went overseas, in fact at Tallahassee that last weekend he knew I was a week late. It's a good thing he did know as one of the girls tells me there are soldiers going across if their wives are pregnant before they go and if they say no and later have a baby they receive no government aid. You know we didn't plan to have one till after the war, so it must have been the hurricane that did it. The date is July 14. Stevie is thrilled to death at the prospect, so someone in the family is tickled anyway. He's planning to take complete charge of it, it sounds like, change diapers, feed it, bathe it, etc. The only thing is we go for a walk with it in the baby carriage he's going to ride his tricycle and have a "parade."

I know it will do Stevie a lot of good, and after all I'm 31 and shouldn't wait too much longer to have more family so it's probably just as well."

"I'm going to let's Stevie handle this baby, hold it, etc. He wants to hold the bottle and help bathe and change diapers, so I'm going to really let him. I think then maybe he'll feel he really has a share and won't be jealous."

"Stevie pulled the good one this evening. He wanted to know how the baby got out of my tummy and I told him the Dr. got him out and he said how, "Does the baby have a key?" You can tell he is really putting some thought to this business."

"The baby has been moving around now for about two weeks and getting more active all the time. I guess it's going to be another live wire!"

"Herald finally agreed to Philip Meredith so that settled, along with Margaret Ann. I went to the doctor today and am fine as usual. I gained 3 pounds this month and now weigh 108. When I started with Stevie I weighed 102 as against 95 this time so don't expect to reach 120 as I did before."

My Father

"About names, since you seem pretty well sold on Kathleen, it's okay with me. Kathy is a nice nickname. Is it ever spelled with a "C"? "

"Mother said the doctor said you could go home on Tuesday and that's today so I suppose you're at the farm now. Phil must be some baby because she says he's the prettiest baby she's ever seen. Of course I suspect a bit of prejudice, don't you. I'm glad he sleeps so well. Doesn't he do a little crying now and then? Surely he must do some?

"Stevie's praying that he was getting into the upper bunk and telling Philip to get his head out of the way so he wouldn't step on it almost put me into convulsions. The little monkey! I'm glad he's pleased that he has a brother since he got what he wanted. Maybe he wouldn't like a sister so well. If the baby looks like you, sweetheart, I'm happy because

I know he's a beautiful baby. But I can't conceive of him being a good baby and not crying."

"She describes Philip as being a plump little boy looking like Stevie was with shapely little ears lifting snugly to his head. And she said you looked very well too. I'm pretty anxious to get a snapshot of our new baby and I'm more anxious to get home and see him for myself."

"I guess I better get some sleep. I hope you are all getting along fine and that the infant formula is agreeing with Philip and that he's gaining and being a good baby."

"So Phil looks likes Stevie according to your dad but you think he has my nose and chin. I hope he does look like Stevie and then we'll be sure to have to two handsome little boys."

"I'm so glad you're feeling well. And I think it's just fine Philip is gaining and not nervous or spits up like Stevie."

"As time goes on we can thank Philip and his 12 points for getting me home sooner."

"I gathered from your letter that Philip hasn't been eating so well and that you had added more water to his formula. I Hope he's okay and guess he must be since you said he was as good as ever."

"One of the large pictures I got today of Mother holding Philip at seven weeks is the best of him yet. I really got a good idea what the little rascal looks like. I think he's a sweet and lovely baby and I'll bet he's even more so now. Gosh he's almost four months old isn't he?"

"Philip is certainly catching on to eating fast, isn't he? Maybe by the time I get back we can get some cute movies of Stevie feeding him."

"The pictures were all good and you and Philip look sweet and lovely, Stevie too for that matter. Philip's got some grin. Gee, but I'm anxious to see him."

"Philip seems to be a very good baby not to cry about being put in the sleeping bag. And he must be a very handsome baby if everyone says he's going to look like Stevie. I Hope he retains a sweet disposition though, don't you?"

I'd certainly like to see Philip lying on his tummy and grinning. Has he rocked back and forth like Stevie did? I'm anxious to see the movies that were taken of him too."

"You know it's going to seem very strange coming back and finding a great big baby boy called Philip. When I left he was slightly more than the glint in his Pappy's eye. I hope I don't frighten him. I'll have to be very gentle and not grab him up right away."

"You mentioned that Philip is playing in the sand. If you can't get trunks small enough for him we'll take him in the water in his diapers or better yet in the nude. We'll start his nude swimming at an early age instead of waiting until after he's married and goes to Minnesota. Wasn't that funny?"

BEFORE I REMEMBER

Since I have very few memories between birth and age four I consulted my baby book, *Our Baby's First Seven Years*, so lovingly kept by my mother.

My nine months in the womb were almost entirely spent in Bradenton Beach, Florida where my mother spent the winters while Dad served overseas during WWII. Just prior to my birth Mother flew back to Indianapolis where I was delivered at the William Coleman Hospital, whose building still stands on the Indiana University Medical Center campus. I was delivered by John F. Spahr, M.D., weighed in at six pounds and seven ounces, and measured 19 ¾ inches in length. My baby book contains my birth announcement telegram sent to my father in France by my grandfather Richman and includes a lock of hair from my first haircut. By age one month I had finally surpassed my birth weight by two ounces. In my baby book I even found my infant formula provided by the Indiana University Medical Center.

Shortly after my birth I was driven to my Grandmother Coons' farm near New Market, in Montgomery County Indiana. Mother lay on the floor with me in the back of the car while my brother Steve watched over back of the front seat. We remained at the farm for two months, and then spent a couple of weeks at the home of Grandma and Grandpa Richman in Columbus, Indiana before flying to Florida. I wish I could recall my first airplane flight!

Mother, Steve, and I remained in Bradenton Beach till my father returned from WWII when I was 8 months old. Our family returned home to Riverview Drive two months later after Dad enjoyed a well-deserved vacation.

I started eating from a spoon at three and a half months, drank from a cup at seven months, and was feeding myself at 12 months...probably with my hands! I started canned vegetable baby food at three and a half months, canned fruits at five and six months, and pureed meats at nine months. I finally conquered the use of a fork at three years of age.

Reportedly my first words were Ma-ma and Da-da at 12 months. I had a "scare" at bowel training at two years and "back-slid." I was probably scared at dropping through the toilet seat hole!

Me as a toddler about to run into the street

Although I was an expert like most kids at taking off my clothes, it wasn't until I was about four years old that I could completely dress myself. I do recall that tying shoelaces was a real chore for me. I was compulsively clean and was washing myself and putting my toys away at three years. I remember getting bathed in the kitchen sink when we lived on Riverview Drive in Indianapolis.

My first haircut at one year was by Mr. Clark at Clark's Barber Shop in the Broad Ripple section of Indianapolis. Although I don't recall this first haircut, I do recall that I was afraid of sitting on the very high board which was placed over the barber chair's arms. I was probably two years of age.

My first neighborhood playmate was Johnny. Later playmates included Douglas, Rodney, Lee, Scott and Janice. My favorite activities by age six or seven included playing cowboys and Indians, riding my trike, playing with blocks and Dinky Toy cars, and climbing trees.

I was a religiously educated kid and my first prayers were "Now I lay me down to sleep," and "Jesus tender shepherd hear me." I knew the Lord's Prayer by age three and a half and started attending Sunday school at the First Presbyterian Church in Indianapolis at age four.

I had my share of childhood illnesses brought home to me from school by my dear brother Steve. These included mumps, chickenpox and measles. I have vague memories of having had the chickenpox.

I recall that my first "doll" (now known as a transitional object in psychoanalytic terms) was a white stuffed doggy which I carried everywhere. The first birthday that I recall was age four when I received a chain-drive bicycle with training wheels. Boy was I proud of graduating from my tricycle! I finally learned to ride without the training wheels when I was age six or seven when we lived in Sherwood Village. Another great accomplishment!

LIVING ON RIVERVIEW DRIVE

Our house on Riverview Drive

I remember only snatches of my first six years when I lived on Riverview Drive in Indianapolis. It's mostly what psychologists call flashbulb memories. I've listed them in no particular order:

> My mother showing me a robin and her eggs in a nest outside her bedroom window

> Watching my mother use the old ringer washing machine in the basement and hanging the clothing on a clothesline

> Getting bathed in the kitchen sink

> Using "bathroom talk" and getting my mouth washed out with soap in the kitchen. I can remember the foul yucky taste.

Observing my brother's Cub Scout meetings in the basement

Sitting on the floor in our living room and watching Howdy Doody, Kukla, Fran and Ollie, and Arthur Godfrey on our first black and white TV

Driving a pedal car and riding a tricycle down the sidewalk in front of our house

Getting my first bike with training wheels. I was so proud to graduate from my trike!

Bleeding like a stuffed pig when my wagon turned over on a small hill. My knee still bears the scar.

Arriving home with my family after a winter vacation to Florida. I awoke just as we pulled into the driveway and I noticed that my stuffed dog needed replacement. I called him "doggie." How original! Doggie was my transitional object. My other dolls included Frank and Baby-Bee.

Sleeping on my stomach in bed

Playing with my Jack-in-the-Box and set of blocks in my bedroom

My most vivid memory was spying a set of weather balloons on the ground just down the street from our house. Johnny, a playmate, was with me and I pointed it out to him. We raced to the balloons, but he arrived first and took possession. His mother made him share them with me. What a lesson in sharing. Although I didn't think so at the time, Johnny's mother was a very wise woman.

T&A

It's not what you think! For that you have to skip a few chapters.

I was five years old and had been sporadically attending Mrs. Cook's Kindergarten because of recurrent colds and ear infections. Upon Dr. Hippensteel's advice my parents decided that I would have my tonsils and adenoids removed. So off I went to Methodist Hospital.

The anesthesiologist placed a mask over my nose and mouth and started dripping ether. "It smells," I said, and I was quickly out.

My next recall is awakening from a dream. It was in Technicolor and ended with a cartoon train rounding a curve and disappearing in the distance, and as it did, Bugs Bunny announced, "That's all folks!"

That afternoon I remember eating ice cream which soothed my sore throat and delighted my taste buds. Oh, the perks of being sick!

That night I had to pee. No way was I going to call for a nurse and have her watch while I peed in a bedpan or urinal. So I climbed out of my high-railed crib and went to the bathroom. A night nurse made me as I was climbing back into the crib.

The next day Dad drove me home from the hospital. I recall an overwhelming wave of nausea and barfing on the floor of the car. I thought Dad would be mad but he was all understanding. He was like that.

A MEMORABLE MEAL

When I was about four years old my parents took Dad's mother, my brother Steve, and me to the Crawfordsville Country Club for dinner. I don't recall what got into me (probably the devil), but I crawled under the table and started to tease my older brother. We must have raised considerable commotion because Steve was thoroughly embarrassed and my father was exasperated, although he didn't show it until our ride back to Grandmother Coons' house. He stopped alongside the gravel road, got out, and preceded to the fence. "What's wrong with Daddy," I asked mother." Before she could answer, I could hear retching from the direction of the fence…and then I knew, or at least I knew that he was throwing up. Years later, after seeing kids act up in restaurants and watching their parents' embarrassment and discomfort, I fully understood.

Well, that's not the end of the story. It seems that the commotion that Steve and I made caused our parents to have a serious conversation which resulted in the following solution: Until I was about age twelve, my brother and I were never allowed to go to a restaurant together with my parents. I recall many fine dinners at the Dennison Restaurant at 54th and College in Indianapolis with just my parents. They always had cocktails before dinner and I was always treated to a "kiddie cocktail," coke served in a cocktail glass containing a cherry on a toothpick.

CHAPTER 2

KINDERGARTEN AND GRADE SCHOOL

"My fondest memory of the first grade at Nora was a litter of new-born puppies which was brought to class by the teachers."

MRS. COOK'S KINDERGARTEN AND SCHOOL 84

I attended Mrs. Cook's Kindergarten on Central Avenue in Indianapolis for a year and a half. I missed so much of the first year because of repeated sore throats and ear infections that my parents thought it best for me to attend a second session after my tonsillectomy. I recall little of the kindergarten class, including students and activities, but I do have a photograph of the entire class. The building in which kindergarten was held still stands, but it is no longer a kindergarten.

Mrs. Cook's Kindergarten, circa 1950

Interestingly I met an alumnus of Mrs. Cook's through my current Sunday school class at North United Methodist Church. My fellow churchgoer reports he was thrown out of kindergarten and just smiles when asked to give specifics. What type of behavior would get a five-year-old boy expelled from kindergarten in the 1940s? My fertile imagination is working overtime on this one!

Prior to moving to Sherwood Village from Riverview Drive, I attended the first semester of the first grade at School 84 in Indianapolis. This school still stands on East 57ᵗʰ Street. It was built with brick and made to last. It is now the Joseph J. Bingham Indianapolis Public School No. 84 and is on the National Register of Historic Places, unlike my second and third grade school buildings which have been demolished.

Like Mrs. Cook's Kindergarten my memories of this grade school are few and far between. I do recall playing percussion in music class and really enjoying it. I also recall with some embarrassment getting sick and barfing on the head of a fellow student in this class. We were both sent home - he to change clothes and me to stay until I felt better.

I also recall that while I was in the first grade a student in another class died from a congenital heart defect. He had been one of the "blue babies" born in the 1940s prior to the advent of corrective heart surgery. I learned about his demise from my brother when I had gone home for lunch that day. When classes resumed in the afternoon our teacher started to tell our class about the tragedy. I tried to add my two cents worth, but was quickly shushed by the teacher. In those days school counseling after tragedies was unknown.

NORA GRADE SCHOOL

My parents moved to Sherwood Village in North Central Indianapolis in the fall of 1951 so my brother and I could attend Washington Township schools. I was enrolled in the first grade at Nora Grade School with Mrs. Mary Castle as my teacher. She had a female teacher's aide whose name I cannot recall. Mrs. Castle was a warm motherly woman, just perfect for a first grade teacher. My fondest memory of the first grade at Nora was a litter of new-born puppies which was brought to class by the teachers. They were so young that their eyes were closed when we first glimpsed them. Days later they opened their eyes and began to get rambunctious.

Mrs. Castle's first grade class, Nora Grade School, circa 1951

We were on a satisfactory/unsatisfactory grading system and I received all satisfactories at Nora Grade School. Comments indicate that my reading and writing had improved and that I could "write good stories," a harbinger of things to come? My teacher in the second grade was Mary Gilliland, and although she made no comments on my report card, I received all satisfactories.

A few years later my Boy Scout Troop met at Nora Grade School. I can still recall the cold dark winter nights when our troop convened.

Sadly, the Nora Grade School I attended no longer exists. It was a four or five story building off Westfield Boulevard just south of 86th Street. It was ultimately torn down to make way for a shopping center and the first North Central High School.

SHERWOOD VILLAGE

In November, 1951 my family moved to Sherwood Village (now a part of Meridian Hills) in northern Indianapolis. Its boundaries were 73rd Street on the north, 71st Street on the south, College Avenue on the west, and Williams Creek Drive on the east. With that move my brother and I changed from Indianapolis Public School #84 to the Washington Township School system and we were both enrolled at Nora Grade School.

Our house on Sherwood Drive

Not long after we moved to the neighborhood some neighbor boys arranged a "fight" between a boy my age and me. Apparently this was a neighborhood initiation ritual. We wrestled a little and then as we both rose to our feet, I kicked him. "You kick," he shouted, and he ran home. How was I to know that kicking was not allowed as I was determined to win this first fight of mine? We waited about 20 minutes for him to return, but he never did, so we all dispersed and went home. That was my first and only fight. Since I was slightly built, I was determined to excel in another area such as academics.

Sherwood Village was a perfect neighborhood in which to grow up. It was small enough to know practically every family and there were lots of kids my age or close to my age. Halloweens were the most fun as many of us kids managed to hit nearly every house and we brought home shopping bags full of treats...the unhealthy variety. And this was before the time that anyone had thought of tampering with Halloween goodies.

There were a few neighborhood "hoods" or JDs who were always in trouble. One or two even got sent off to the Culver Military Academy to straighten them out. I tried to stay away from these bullies.

I had my share of playmates. Two of my favorites, Rodney and Douglas, lived one street over from our street on Nottingham Court. We spent many hours playing with Dinky Toy cars, the forerunners of Hot Wheels, in each other's gravel driveways. Two other playmates, Scott and Janice, were brother and sister who lived right next door. We passed many hours playing Cowboys and Indians and Hide and Seek.

A nearby woods extended north and south along Williams Creek and many of us boys built forts there and created tunnels in the sand by digging a trench, overlaying it with boards, and then covering it all with sand. We also built tree houses overlooking the creek.

Williams Creek was known to flood. Accordingly, there were several occasions during our eight years there that the water crept up to low spots on Williams Creek Drive and flooded basements, including ours, which was closest house on Sherwood Drive to the creek. I recall that a neighbor rented a big pump to pump out flooded basements. During the pumping the neighbor men would stand around, smoke, and drink beer.

We had great neighbors. Dr. Bertram Roth, who lived just across the street from us, was my pediatrician. When my father unwisely tried to clear the grass from his rotary lawn mower and sliced off part of his thumb, it was Dr. Roth who stitched him up in his office in Broad Ripple. The Trusty family lived just next door and our parents remained friends with them for many years after we moved from Sherwood Village. The Tuchman family of Indianapolis dry cleaner fame lived on the other side of us. The Land family lived just behind us and their son Bill was my brother's age. I recall that they had a female hunting dog and were rather upset while our male dachshund tried to mount her through the backyard fence. They wanted no mixed-breed puppies to be born to their prized hunting dog.

Summer times were glorious as school was out and we kids got to play outside much of the time. Mother's only rule was that we had to be back indoors when darkness fell. Mom even had a bell which she rang to summon us home at dinnertime.

One of our summertime activities was rather unhealthy in retrospect. Since we were just about 50 yards from Williams Creek, mosquitoes were a nuisance. A local service sprayed our neighborhood with a mosquito-killing substance. It was sprayed from a jeep with the spraying apparatus mounted on the back. We little kids would race behind the jeep and jump in and out of the fog that it produced. I do recall that several parents wondered if this mosquito fog might be harmful, but nothing was ever done to prevent our activity. Now I shudder to think what toxic chemicals might have been in that mosquito fog.

I hated to leave my school, my playmates, and Sherwood Village behind when our family moved to Puerto Rico in the summer of 1959, but it was on to a new adventure that I will never forget.

DELAWARE TRAIL GRADE SCHOOL

I attended Delaware Trail Grade School from the third through the sixth grades. Delaware Trail replaced Nora Grade School which was demolished to build a shopping center. Eventually Delaware Trail was demolished to construct an apartment complex, so of the three grade schools that I attended, only Indianapolis Public School #84, the oldest of the three, still exists. A lovely building, it was constructed to last.

Looking back over my school grades I am astonished to see how poorly I performed in the third grade. My grades were mostly Bs and Cs and my deportment was horrible. I was repeatedly cited for talking in class and failing to use my spare time wisely. I do recall being exiled to the hall on a number of occasions as were many of my classmates. Once our principal Mr. Bailey walked down the hall and I remember him shaking his head as he passed a quarter of the class who had been told to "take your desk and sit in the hall," by our teacher, Mrs. Hagans. Fortunately, during the rest of my career at Delaware Trail my grades improved to As and Bs and my deportment was always satisfactory.

My first and only foray into the performing arts occurred at Delaware Trail in the third grade. Because of repression I remember very little, but apparently the third grade was having a variety show. Two other little boys and I dressed up in boxes as outfits and did a little soft-shoe to "Me and My Shadow." Now I can re-repress this horrible memory.

My fondest memories of Delaware Trail, however, were not academic; my favorite "class" was recess. Due to the efforts of our excellent school board, Delaware Trail possessed a wonderful playground which ran the length of the school and was situated immediately behind our elongated building. We had teeter-totters, jungle-jims, swings, slides, monkey-bars, and merry-go-rounds. Unlike the sterile playgrounds of today, our playground surface was pea gravel which made for many scrapes and bruises when we fell off the teeter-totter or parachuted out of the swings. One of my classmates even broke his wrist after participating in this dangerous practice.

I can remember us burning our fannies on the hot slides which had been heated by the noonday sun. I can also recall how we "bumped" each other off the teeter-totters. I remember getting dizzy after spending too much time on the merry-go-round.

My fondest memory is of the two jungle-jims that graced our playground. Somehow the most southern one became the "girls'" jungle-jim and the northernmost was appropriated by the boys. Woe to the little girl or boy who tried to get on the jungle-jim of the opposite sex. We boys and girls would chase each other from one jungle-jim to the other. Back and forth we gangs of girls and boys ran, chasing one another, screaming all the way. I liked that playground so much that I almost didn't want to graduate to the seventh grade at Westlane Junior High School.

THE DOGHOUSE

I was never much for running away and hiding and I'll tell you why.

Once in childhood I was mad at my mother and told her I planned to run away from home. "Fine," she said, "I'll help you pack your bags." Well, that really took the wind out of my sails! She was one smart mother!

On another occasion my brother and I rode the bus home from Nora Grade School. My brother was in the fifth grade and I was in the first. We never sat together on the bus and Steve was sitting far in front of me and got off first. We always got off on Nottingham Court and took a shortcut home through a neighbor's back yard, over a fence, and into our back yard. We would enter the house through the back door which was always unlocked because Mother was home. Since Steve had a long head-start, he arrived first, went in and locked the door. Mother asked Steve where I was and he said he didn't know. She asked him if I'd been on the bus and he said he didn't know even though I'd been close on his tail after getting off the bus. Mother began to get upset and called two boys in the neighborhood who were also in first grade. They couldn't remember if I was on the bus. She called the school and talked to the principal and also to my teacher. They went out and checked the parking lot and looked around the school and found no sign of me. They said they'd check with the school bus driver when he was through with his route. By this time Mother was getting frantic and was wondering what to do next. Fortunately, before she did anything more, she heard pounding on the door and upon opening it, found me. I was mad as a wet hen and barked, "Steve locked me out!" She asked me where I had been while she was making all those calls and I said, "I was in Sandy's dog house."

As I recall, I banged loudly on the back door when I first arrived, but no one heard me. I tried the back door to the garage, but it too was locked. Finally, in desperation, because it was a somewhat chilly spring day, I crawled into our dog Sandy's doghouse and angrily commenced to pout and plot revenge. I don't know how long I pouted, maybe two hours. Eventually, pangs of hunger got to me. I knocked on the door and was let in by Mother. Years later Mother said, "I can't believe it was that long, or I'd have called the sheriff, the state police and FBI."

Come to think of it, I never did get my revenge! And I've never been in a literal doghouse again, but I've been in my wife's doghouse of disapproval, or so she says!

SUMMER CAMP

When I was a child I attended two Indiana summer camps, Acorn Farm Camp in Hamilton County and Gnaw Bone Camp in Brown County.

My brother Steve preceded me at Acorn Farm Camp. I remember attending a family picnic there when I was age four or five. As soon as I got up on their red fire truck and climbed around I knew I had to attend this camp. Of course, it was painted fire engine red!

Acorn Farm Camp was a coed day camp and an old yellow school bus came take me there every morning. I can still recall the cool morning air as I waited to be picked up in front of my home in Sherwood Village in Indianapolis. The camp was run by Herb and Dee Sweet and their two daughters, Jill and Judee, served as two of the camps many counselors. Activities included making dams and hunting for crawdads in Cool Creek, climbing trees, riding the Sky Slide, an early form of a zip line, hiking, pony rides, swimming, fire-building, and engaging in various crafts.

Prior to the installation of a swimming pool on the camp property, campers would travel on a bus to Northern Woods Beach in Carmel. At camp lunches were served in a screened-in dining hall. Menus generally consisted of PB&J sandwiches and "bug juice" (Cool-Aid). Afterwards we would all sit in rapt attention listening to stories and nature talks given by Mr. Sweet.

After attending Acorn Farm Camp for several years from about age six to age nine, I graduated to Gnaw Bone Camp where male campers stayed overnight for one or two weeks. I had never been away from home for that length of time, and although I didn't get homesick, I can recall several campers who did and had to leave early.

Me facing the camera at Gnaw Bone Camp in Brown County, Indiana

At Gnaw Bone we engaged in many of the same activities in which we'd participated at Acorn Farm Camp. Every nice afternoon we were driven in an open-air truck to a reservoir about five miles away. The swimmers could swim out to a pontoon raft and spend the afternoon diving off it or getting a suntan. Evenings were usually spent around a campfire while we sang and roasted marshmallows. S'mores had not made it to Gnaw Bone when I attended. Darn it! We also were told ghost stories by the camp counselors. My favorite was about the Brown County Monster, a forerunner of Bigfoot.

Camp meals were served in a large dining hall. Lunches and dinners always included bug juice. At dinner and after dinner we were encouraged not to imbibe too much liquid to avoid "floating" in our bunks.

Sleeping accommodations were provided in one of eight or ten screened-in cabins. Flaps could be rolled down on the sides of the cabins in case of rain. I cannot recall precisely how many campers were allotted to each cabin. I think it was six or eight. Outdoor privies were provided where we could relieve ourselves.

I have a few favorite memories of having attended Gnaw Bone Camp for two or three years. On one occasion we boys formed several "companies" and made sassafras tea, gallons and gallons of the stuff. We hunted and dug up the sassafras roots which were plentiful on the property, built a fire, and then boiled the sassafras. It made great tea and we often enjoyed it at dinnertime.

Another memory is of taking some tenderfoot campers in my cabin to the Haunted House to stay all night. This house was an abandoned two-story home about a mile away from camp. To reach it we had to follow a rutted road from the edge of camp property. About four of us arrived at the Haunted House around dusk and we proceeded to roll out our sleeping bags on the floor in a second story room. Of course, this seasoned camper had to tell the other campers about the Brown County Monster. Afterwards we lay down in our bedrolls and tried to go to sleep. There wasn't anything else to do because we wanted to preserve the batteries in our flashlights. We listened to the whippoorwills calling in the night. Pretty soon we began to hear strange sounds, bumping and groaning of the floor boards. Had the Brown County Monster entered the house? We weren't going to stay around and find out, so we packed up our bedrolls and rapidly walked back to our warm bunks at camp.

LAKE TIPPECANOE

For a number of years in the early 1950s our family vacationed at Lake Tippecanoe in Kosciusko County, Indiana. We stayed at the historic Stony Ridge Hotel on the south shore of the lake. Sadly, this hotel fell into disrepair and was torn down to make way for new vacation homes. Directly across the lake we could see the Tippecanoe Lake Country Club. Just down the sidewalk to the east of the hotel was the Lake Tippy Dance Hall, a historic site, which still exists and is in full operation on summer weekends. The south side of the lake was lined with summer homes and vacation rentals. It was fun to walk down the sidewalk to the dance hall and marina. Many homes had piers out front as well as purple martin bird houses atop tall poles.

Our hotel had a pier and rowboats that were free of charge to hotel patrons. Although it was fun to use the rowboat, I longed to ride in a sleek speedboat. To my chagrin and embarrassment, Dad had a one and a half horsepower trolling motor which he attached to the rowboat. It propelled us at about two miles an hour, not nearly fast enough for a six-year-old boy.

One of my favorite memories was our lake excursions on an old steam-powered paddlewheel boat. The trip to Little Tippecanoe Lake and back took several hours. On one trip the boat broke down and we had to be rescued by speedboats. The long wait for rescue filled me with anxiety. After the boat had been repaired my parents and brother took another trip on the boat. Too scared to take another trip on that boat and risk being stranded again, I stayed at the hotel with my grandmother Coons. While they were away I was sitting on the screened porch with my grandmother when a huge summer thunderstorm blew up. The rain and wind were furious and the wind-driven rain all but obscured the lake. Thunder and lightning were all around. With each loud clap of thunder I imagined my parents drowning as the paddle-wheeler sank out of sight. Abundant tears were freely flowing as my grandmother tried to console me. Eventually the storm abated, the sun came out, and my parents returned several hours later, none the worse for wear.

Our family photo archives have a number of pictures of our activities at Lake Tippecanoe. We liked to jump off the end of the pier, swim, splash each other, and float around on inner tubes and rubber rafts. Mother was into sun bathing and my brother and I got fabulous suntans. Several of our photos depict my Aunt Frances and Uncle Bruce Johnson who visited us at Stony Ridge with their children, Judy and Greg.

My mother and me, "String-bean," sitting in one of the rowboats provided by the Stony Ridge Hotel

Although I've returned several times to Lake Tippy to visit, things just aren't the same without the old Stony Ridge Hotel. I guess one can never truly return to the carefree days of childhood.

CHAPTER 3

JUNIOR HIGH AND HIGH SCHOOL

"I recall our female world history teacher who would stand on a stage and lecture, sometimes with her eyes half-closed and eyelids fluttering. We used to joke with each other that she appeared to be in a trance."

WESTLANE JUNIOR HIGH SCHOOL

I spent the seventh and eighth grades at Westlane Junior High School in Indianapolis. Newly built, it was one of the first junior high schools in the city. Although it has been enlarged, today it looks much as it did in 1957 when I first attended.

I had several memorable teachers at Westlane. The first was Arnold Spilly who taught United States history. Mr. Spilly kindled my life-long interest in American history.

My science teacher, John Van Sickle was a legend at Westlane. He was an incredible inspiration who awoke my interest in science. A slender man, he used to sit in a lotus position on his desk. After the school day had ended for a precise amount of time he was always available to parents and students who came to his classroom. He came up with a phrase to help us recall the order of the planets in our solar system. Mr. (Mercury) Vansickle (Venus) eats (Earth), Mars-bars (Mars), and jelly (Jupiter), sandwiches (Saturn), under (Uranus), (Neptune), porch (Pluto). I'm afraid I cannot recall what Neptune stood for (probably next-door) but I've never forgotten the order of the planets. Unfortunately Pluto was dropped as a planet in 2006 and is now a dwarf planet named plutoid.

I had a solid B average while at Westlane and that's where I learned to study. There I learned that checking my work during tests was essential if I wanted to make a good grade.

As I recall we didn't have recess or a playground at Westlane. We did have an excellent gymnasium where we were exposed to rope climbing, calisthenics, including jumping jacks and pushups, and the use of the parallel bars and the pommel horse. I did not participate in team sports because of my low weight and poor eye-hand coordination.

Sadly, I had to leave Westlane and not have the ninth grade there since my family moved to Puerto Rico. I missed all of my friends whom I had known since the first grade, but was on to a new adventure.

GLASSES, BRACES, AND ACNE, OR FOUR-EYES, METAL-MOUTH, AND PIMPLE-FACE

My skinny body wasn't my only problem as a child and adolescent. In the fourth grade I discovered by closing one eye and then the other and looking at a distant pattern, there was a difference in my vision. I reported this to my mother and I soon found myself at the ophthalmologist's office and not long thereafter I had my first pair of glasses. Glasses were a mixed blessing, however. Although I could now see the blackboard at school, I was now known as "four-eyes," according to my empathetic brother.

Around the same time, my parents arranged for me to be fitted with braces because I had an overbite or "buck teeth." I also had a small mouth which required the extraction of four permanent canine teeth, so my desire to be a vampire with long fangs was forever dashed. Braces were a mixed blessing. My monthly dental visits allowed me to be away from classes for a couple of hours, but there were several days of pain involved from having my braces tightened. Think of brace tightening as being the dental equivalent of the medieval torture rack and you'll have a proper picture of what this involves.

Me and my braces in the third grade

Then there were the frequent jokes about kissing a girl with braces and getting your two sets of braces entangled. In fact, John Grogan in his memoir, *The Longest Trip Home*, described his first French kiss with a girl thusly, "French kissing with Lori was a little like French kissing a power tool. I spent half the time marveling at my amazing luck and the other half trying to prevent serious injury." Fortunately for me, I had most of my braces removed before I attempted to engage in this advanced kissing technique. The less fortunate Grogan reported a highly noticeable abrasion just above his upper lip.

Of course, there were the usual wise cracks about people wearing braces. "Metal mouth" was the most common.

Folks who haven't worn braces haven't heard the lingo that accompanies the orthodontic technique of correcting malocclusion. First, metal brackets are glued to the teeth and then these brackets are wired together. The ultimate goal is to pull or jack the individual teeth into proper alignment. I wore an "appliance" at night. This device almost defies description. Metal processes hook into each side of the upper braces and an attached semicircular metal rod extends outside the mouth. The whole contraption is held in place by an elastic band which wraps around the neck. Small rubber bands are inserted inside the mouth to keep the upper and lower jaws in close approximation. Wearing this type of contraption makes it all but impossible to French kiss. Eating with this is impossible and speech is slurred. This is the dental equivalent of a chastity belt. After the braces were finally removed, I wore a plastic retainer on the palate to keep the upper teeth in alignment.

My final indignity to childhood and adolescence, and early adulthood was the development of acne or an impressive collection of pimples, whiteheads, blackheads, papules, pustules, and nodules. And, of course, this had to occur at the onset of my dating career. Who wants to accept a date with a pimply-faced teen? So, what did my mother do? She sent me to a dermatologist and I was prescribed an endless number of soaps, creams, lotions, astringents, antibiotics, and hormones. I even got estrogens!

I finally grew out of adolescence and suppressed these childhood and adolescent indignities until just now. Please allow me to put them out of my mind again.

BOY SCOUTS

I joined the Cub Scouts in the first grade. My mother was a Cub Scout den mother for me just as she had been for my brother Steve. I advanced to the Boy Scouts as soon as I was eligible; I think around age 10 or 11. For me the hardest rank to achieve was First Class because I had to learn the Morse Code and I was not good at memorization. However, I finally did make First Class along with many of my scouting buddies. Later on I achieved Star rank which required six merit badges and finally Life rank which required five more merit badges. I cannot recall all of my merit badges but know that I had badges in cooking, cycling, first aid, athletics, camping, hiking, lifesaving, and swimming. I gained a number of these merit badges under the tutelage of Jim Gregory while I was a camper at Gnaw Bone Camp in Brown County, Indiana.

Part of Indianapolis Boy Scout Troop 117

My fondest memories of the Boy Scouts were of the camping trips that we took at least twice a year. We went on "Shiverees" at Camp Rotary in Montgomery County in the middle of winter. Fortunately we camped inside a building heated with a pot-bellied stove. During summers we would go to Camp Belzer on the east side of Indianapolis. It was at Belzer that I flunked my rowing test when I was unable to row a 250-pound counselor up Fall Creek against the current. I became so flummoxed that I couldn't recall which side of the boat was port and which side was starboard.

My most memorable experience was when many in our troop hiked the Ten O'clock Line Trail which leads from Yellowwood Lake in Yellowwood State Forest and ends at the fire tower in Brown County State Park. It was a rigorous 16-mile hike which took all day.

We camped out on Friday night prior to starting the hike and it was so cold that many of us could not sleep even though we should have had adequate sleeping bags. We hiked up and down hills and, as we were doing so, I often looked longingly down in the valley and wished that we could follow the obviously flat gravel roads that I saw below us. At noon we rested and ate lunch. The mother of one fellow hiker had packed his lunch in glass jars which added to the weight of his already heavy pack. I thanked God that I had packed my lunch in sandwich bags. We arrived at the end of our hike near dusk and had to follow a compass route up to the fire tower. We were all exhausted by the time we had reached the endpoint of our journey. It was a hike that I will never forget.

I was forced to give up scouting when our family moved to Puerto Rico just after I finished the eighth grade. One of my greatest regrets is that I did not pick up scouting again when our family moved back to Indiana when I was 15, so I was never able to attain the rank of Eagle Scout like my brother Steve. My budding interest in girls undid any interest I had in scouting. The cute blonde girl who lived across the street from me was no help! I decided that it was more fun to chat with her after school than pursue more merit badges.

ST. JOHN'S PREPARATORY SCHOOL

While I lived in Puerto Rico during the ninth grade (1959-1960) I attended St. John's Preparatory School, now known simply as St. John's School. It was located one block from the Atlantic Ocean in the Condado Beach neighborhood in Santurce, a suburb immediately adjacent to Old San Juan. St. John's classes included K-12th grade and teaching was in English with the exception of Spanish class.

During my tenure at St. John's there was no air conditioning, but trade-wind breezes frequently came through the open doors and louvered windows of the classrooms. Lunch was eaten outside on picnic tables and those who wanted to could venture just off campus for snow-cones available in a myriad of exotic flavors.

I recall that we wore uniforms. We boys wore white shirts and khaki or navy slacks and the girls wore white blouses and khaki or navy skirts.

My courses included algebra, Spanish, English, study skills, and world history. I made high Bs and ranked fourth in a class of 30.

Every morning either my father or a couple of other fathers would drive three of us from Rio Piedras, another San Juan suburb where we lived, to St. John's. I remember Bob, a classmate's father, sometimes getting irritated when a *Puertorriqueña* driver pulled out in front of us, as many were wont to do. "You want to get yourself killed," he would yell, apparently not understanding that most *Puertorriqueña* drivers could not understand English. At least it made him feel better.

I have several salient memories from attending St. John's. One is of our male headmaster's favorite saying, "Experience is a tough school but fools will learn in no other." How true. I recall our female world history teacher who would stand on a stage and lecture, sometimes with her eyes half-closed and eyelids fluttering. We used to joke with each other that she appeared to be in a trance. I think we were right.

Still another memory is of a female classmate from Connecticut. Once we were staffing the snack-bar where we sold drinks and candy bars to classmates, and I remarked to her how hot it was and that I was "sweating up a storm." Nose in the air, she retorted, "Horses sweat. Humans perspire." She put me in my place. "How dare she?" I thought. I'd never known anyone from Connecticut before, especially one that put on airs like that. How was a Hoosier boy like me to know?

My final memory of St. John's is that we were offered a sex education course over a two day period. I think this was unusual for a school at this time, especially for a school with Lutheran connections. The boys and girls were split up and the grades were split into two classes, one for grades 10-12 and one for grades 7-9. Most of what was taught I had already heard, but one piece of misinformation was fed to us boys in grades 7-9: We shouldn't masturbate because you only had a certain number of lifetime shots stored within you. I wonder what the girls were told and if it was that inaccurate.

St. John's was a wonderful school academically. I learned how to study there, preparing me well for New Albany Senior High School.

NEW ALBANY SENIOR HIGH SCHOOL

After moving back to Indiana at the end of the ninth grade, our family located in New Albany, Indiana. In grades ten through twelve I attended New Albany Senior High School. The first year we lived in New Albany we lived in a rented house on Captain Frank Road until my parents located a suitable house to buy. Eventually they found a two bedroom, one bath home on Riddle Road in the Silver Hills section of New Albany, high on a hill above the rest of the city. Our home was located at the west end of Riddle Road and had a magnificent view of the hills to the west.

Our home on Riddle Road in New Albany, Indiana

I started high school as a sophomore and felt rather lost at first because I had no friends and most of the other classmates had been together since grade school. I had to attend summer school the first year to take make up a physical education course that I had missed while living in Puerto Rico.

Gradually I made friends including a number from the Silver Hills neighborhood. One good friend, Tom, I met in home room and we shared an avid interest in Ernest Hemingway. Another two friends, Karen and Jack, lived immediately across the street, but they attended Providence, the local Catholic high school.

I was surprised to learn of a number of fraternities and sororities for high school students but these were not associated or sanctioned by the high school. I eventually joined the Dysphorians, so named because we were saddened because we were not chosen as members of the other fraternities. I recall that we Dysphorians went to some out-of-town high school basketball and football games and built a float for the New Albany Sesquicentennial in 1963. I got rather sick to my stomach while building the float because we all smoked cigars to try to be cool. Alcohol and drugs were not part of my high school experience, thank goodness!

I did well academically in senior high school, graduating 21st out of a class of 410, and received six Scholarship Ns, similar to athletic letters, for doing well in academics. I am unaware if other high schools offered letters for academics during this time period. I think it was a definite plus that New Albany Senior High School, the first high school in the state of Indiana, offered academic letters. I made straight As except for 4 Bs during six grading periods in English during my junior year. In spite of that, English was one of my favorite subjects and I recall with fondness all of my English teachers including Mrs. Tyler, Mr. Wardell, and Mr. Lamb. Mr. Lamb taught us all the "dirt" regarding the British poets and authors.

During my high school years I was a member of a number of school clubs including the Spanish Club, the Wranglers (a boys' debate society), the National Honor Society, and the Student Council. I recall that the initiation ritual for the Wranglers was to eat a block of Limburger cheese, a can of Spinach and chase those with a glass of vinegar. It was not my idea of a great meal, but it was my introduction to hazing, of which I would see more in college.

I was a good kid in high school and did not rebel. The most rebellious thing I participated in was to wear a tie to class one day. All of us boys decided to rebel by wearing ties and there was nothing the school administration could do to object.

While I was in high school I had a moderate case of acne and was rather thin, and since I was somewhat shy, I was fearful of asking young ladies for dates. Although I did eventually have dates with various women in high school, I can still painfully recall phoning them to ask them out. I would shut myself in my parents' bedroom and build up enough courage over about five minutes to call a girl while my heart pounded and beat wildly in my chest. I was in abject fear of being turned down, and I was more times than I like to remember. I did date a very sweet young woman during my senior year but once we went off to separate colleges separated by 80 miles, our relationship did not last. Although I did well academically in high school, because of my shyness, adolescence was an awkward time for me.

SILVER HILLS OR THE "HILL"

Silver Hills is located at the southern end of a series of hills or "knobs" which extended from New Albany on the Ohio River north almost sixty miles. Most folks are in agreement that the name Silver Hills was derived from the silver poplars that grew in the woods on the south end of the knobs. The neighborhood of Silver Hills was mostly unpopulated until the late nineteenth century when a scenic electric streetcar line was constructed. This line snaked its way horizontally around the side of the Hill on its way to the crest of this steep knob. The construction of the streetcar line and the addition of electric lights made Silver Hills a popular place to go to view the lights of Louisville and soon the land was subdivided and homes began to sprout up all over the Hill. Earlier in the nineteenth century the New Albany Waterworks had constructed a series of reservoirs on the Hill which supplied water under pressure to the West End of New Albany. Another site of interest on the Hill was the Silver Hills Camp Ground which hosted yearly religious revivals.

In 1961 when I was a sophomore in high school my family moved to Silver Hills. Our house, a two bedroom, one-story brick home, was at the west end of Riddle Road and overlooked a valley to the west through which Corydon Pike ran. A series of knobs was on the other side of the valley. Sunsets from our living room or the attached porch were always magnificent and Mother often invited neighbors to come view the sunset and share an evening toddy.

We had wonderful neighbors. Directly across the street from us lived Emma Gohmann, her Catholic priest son and her daughter Martha with her two children. On one side of Emma's house lived Maude and Mort Higgins with Maude's sister Blanche. On the other side lived Wiley Ellis and his family (more about them later). These three families along with ours constituted the entire population of the west end of Riddle Road. On the east end of Riddle Road lived Sherman Minton, a former Democratic Senator from Indiana and Associate United States Supreme Court Justice.

The homes on the south side of Riddle Road all had a magnificent view of the Ohio River and the west end of Louisville. Unfortunately the view to one's right was marred by the smoke stacks of a large coal-burning power plant which was built in the late 50s and early 60s. Fine ash from the stacks rained down constantly and covered cars, patio furniture, etc.

Access to Silver Hills was provided by a number of streets. Cherry Street Hill provided a steep straight shot to the top as did Camp Avenue. Access from Crestwood, an adjacent subdivision, was provided via Old Vincennes Road which ran past Silvercrest, an old TB sanitarium. Spring Street Hill provided the most direct route from downtown New Albany. This road was sinuous and tortuously steep and in recent years has often been closed due to frequent landslides and washouts. Main Street Hill provided another access but this route had many switchbacks and was full of potholes. Now it is closed and overgrown by plants and fallen trees.

The Hill was populated with numerous young families with many children. There was a large vacant lot where we children played softball and two tennis courts where neighbors and their friends played tennis. On rainy days we teens would congregate in the attic of the Ellis garage to play cards and ping pong.

On foggy nights it was fun and a little bit spooky to walk down Highland Avenue past Greystone Gables, a huge stone mansion surrounded by a four-foot stone wall. This home, originally built by Col. E.V Knight in 1912, was owned by Karl and Margaret Moser when I lived on the Hill.

A little bit further along Highland Avenue, it curved around the Waterworks. During my tenure on the Hill, the Waterworks had a two-story stone service and equipment building. The reservoirs themselves were surrounded by a high chain-link fence topped with barb wire. The earthen sides of the reservoirs were covered with honeysuckle which during the spring and summer was in full bloom with white flowers exuding a delightful fragrance.

Two streets over from Riddle Road was Ridgeway Avenue which was lined with a series of beautiful Victorian homes. Doc Hess, a prominent New Albany pediatrician, lived on this street with his wife and five children.

My parents continued to live in their house on Riddle Road long after my dad retired. Their tenure on the Hill lasted nearly forty years until their declining health in the late 1990s forced them to move. I still have many fond memories of that home.

UNCLE WILEY AND THE ELLIS CLAN

As soon as we had met he said, "Call me Uncle Wiley." I did and so did all of the other kids who lived in the Silver Hills subdivision which overlooked New Albany, Indiana.

Uncle Wiley, also known as Col. Ellis from his WWII days in the Army Air Corps, had retired from his family-owned fertilizer business in his 40s to raise his family. Prior to his marriage to Margaret Jordan, he had graduated from high school in Louisville, Kentucky and attended Purdue University where he studied engineering and lettered in four sports. The Ellis family lived in a castle-like home on Silver Hills in a spot overlooking the Ohio River and the west end of Louisville.

Wiley, with the help of some friends and neighbors, hand-built a swimming pool next to their house and also put in a clay tennis court directly across the street from their house and immediately adjacent to our house. Flood lights enabled tennis playing at night in almost any season. Everyone in the Ellis family was a tennis player. It was not unremarkable then that all four Ellis children, Jerri, Nancy, Bill, and Charlie, were state champion tennis players in high school.

Although I attempted to learn how to play tennis under Uncle Wiley's tutelage, I had no eye-hand coordination, so Uncle Wiley wisely let me off the hook. It was fun however to watch others play, particularly in mixed doubles. I did learn tennis etiquette from Uncle Wiley. There was to be no obscene language on the tennis court, not even a mild damn. Tennis was a polite sport at that time. Zero was never mentioned as a score. It was always, "love."

There were a number of stories circulating about Uncle Wiley and I was never certain which to believe. I heard that he had flown a plane under the K&I Railroad Bridge over the Ohio River and had passed a car in the narrow breakdown lane on that same bridge. My best sources swore that both stories were true.

While I lived on the Hill, I learned how to drive. One lesson that I learned from Uncle Wiley was to scan the horizon and anticipate traffic one or two blocks ahead. That by now well-ingrained habit has stood the test of time and enabled me to avoid numerous traffic tie-ups.

One of my fondest memories of the Ellis family was during the yearly Christmas caroling party that Wiley's gracious wife Margaret would host. Friends and family would gather on the appointed evening, go sing Christmas carols to neighbors, and then retire to their dining room to feast on punch, cookies, and other delectables.

Uncle Wiley's eldest daughter Jerri was one year ahead of me in high school. My father often drove us across town to high school on many mornings. Jerri was a beautiful young woman and I instantly realized that she was way out of my league, so I didn't even attempt to ask for a date.

Jerri and I did engage in much good-natured banter on the mornings we rode to school together. One morning just prior to my father getting in the car, Jerri told me I had "bedroom eyes." That expression wasn't entirely new to me as my mother had told me the same thing, although with not the same inflection. I felt complemented and told my girlfriend about my bedroom eyes. "Who told you that," she said with a bit of jealously in her voice. I learned a lesson from that experience: Be humble and keep quiet!

DOC ROSE

Lawrence S. Rose was my chemistry teacher during my junior year at New Albany High School (NAHS). Doc had a reputation as a hard ass, perhaps because of his gruff exterior. Juniors taking his college prep chemistry course entered with a sense of foreboding. They'd been forewarned by legions of previous chemistry students.

I entered Doc's class not knowing what to expect, but I took an immediate liking to this gray-haired prof. Those who followed directions and were conscientious had nothing to fear, however, woe to the hapless student who was a goof-off!

One of my favorite memories of Doc's class concerned my classmate Betsy. Like most of the young women in my class, Betsy was somewhat fearful of Doc. On one warm day Betsy had tarried too long at lunch. To avoid being late and incurring Doc's wrath, Betsy decided to climb through the first floor window into our classroom. To the classes utter delight Betsy pulled herself through the window and plopped down into her seat just before Doc entered the room. Betsy scraped her leg but was none the worse for wear.

Despite his gruff exterior, Doc had a heart of gold. He was my homeroom teacher during my junior year and as such he was responsible for handing out tickets to our junior prom which was closed to all except students at NAHS. Somewhere along the line I must have shared my tale of woe that I was dating a student at Providence High School in Clarksville, Indiana. Bless his heart, he provided me with two tickets to the prom.

My prom date and I were neighbors. Also living close by was Mrs. Biggerstaff, who was also a NAHS teacher. It happened that Mrs. Biggerstaff was greeting students and taking tickets on board the Avalon, an Ohio River paddle-wheeler where our prom was held. We were instantly made as we came on board, but we were allowed to stay for the entire prom. I caught grief for it later because I refused to apologize to Mr. Brown, our school principal. I paid dearly for my misdeed and received no senior awards for my excellent grades. But why did I need to apologize? I had simply treated my date to a marvelous evening.

I recall one day during class Doc asked, "Who is interested in geology?" I quickly raised my hand and landed a life-changing opportunity. With Doc's strong recommendation, I was selected along with seven other high school juniors and seniors to attend the Indiana University Geologic Field Station in the Tobacco Root Mountains in southwestern Montana. What a summer that was, but more about that later.

So, here's to you, Doc Rose, my all-time favorite high school teacher. I can't thank you enough for all you did for me.

CHAPTER 4

COLLEGE DAYS

"Dr. Haenisch's nickname was 'Heavy Ed.' It's a little unclear how he acquired his nickname, but some might suspect it was because he was a bit on the heavy side."

Most of the selections in this chapter were written for the website *Wabash Stories*, the brainchild of Bruce Gras, (Wabash, '68). Several of these selections first appeared in my book, *In their own Words: Hoosier ancestor and family journeys* (Bloomington, Indiana: iUniverse, 2009)

PLEDGESHIP

Pledgeship is the period between pledging a fraternity and becoming initiated as a full-time member. In my days at Wabash, pledgeship was physically and mentally demanding. In addition to our house jobs, which mostly included keeping the house clean, there was much physical and mental hazing which culminated in "hell week," a three-day period during semester break in January, where pledges went without sleep for three days and underwent intense hazing.

My attitudes towards hazing and pledgeship changed markedly during my Wabash career and subsequently. Initially I looked on pledgeship with some fear and anticipation and even thought that some of it would be fun. By the end of "hell week" I was about ready to leave the fraternity. As a sophomore I did not participate in hazing and, as a junior, I became very disillusioned with the practice, as the house grade average fell to last place among fraternities, a fact I attributed mostly to pledgeship.

The following are excerpts from letters that I wrote my parents about pledgeship:

September 17, 1963

…So far fraternity life is fine, although pledgeship hasn't started yet. I like one pledge brother in particular. His name is Haines and he is from Downers Grove, Illinois…

September 19, 1963

…We have a fill pledge class of twenty-two now, the best pledge class on campus…

September 25, 1963

…Last Monday night I was elected president of my pledge class and last night pledgeship started in earnest. It was quite a shock to us all.

I only hope that I can keep up enough courage and stamina to pull us all through. It's going to be very difficult...My roommates are Bob and Stu. They're really taking care of me. I just finished doing eight pushups for a slight offense. Many of the rules are asinine, and sometimes there is very little time to study, but I guess it's worth it in the long run...

October 11, 1963

...So far this week has been uneventful except for a very tough [pledge] line. I've been working my butt off. Sometimes I get the feeling that I ought to call it quits, but the feeling quickly passes...

October 18, 1963

...This week has been a tough one. I barely have enough time to do my house job and complete my homework. Of course, I have time to associate with my pledge brothers, but I never have any time to sit down and think or go out for a walk and enjoy the fall colors.

This week my house job has been mail boy. I enjoy it because I ride a bicycle and Wooglin [the fraternity dog] follows alongside me. I dread to think of what it will be like in cold weather, though...

October 25, 1963

...We had our second big line of the year last Thursday night. It was a "midnight snack" Of course we had to work up a good appetite, so we ran up and down the stairs about five times. The meal consisted of crackers, all they could stuff in our mouths, and butter, about ½ stick, vinegar to drink, and onions for dessert. Not a bad meal at all. I'm looking forward to our sixteen course dinner...

January 7, 1964

...I want to be home as long as possible before "hell week" begins, probably Wednesday of the next week...

Thus far everything has been pretty quiet and I expect it to remain so until "hell week." Down in the basement the sophomores have put up a chart, "Hell via Route 66." I expect that I'll build up quite a lot of mileage between now and "hell week"…

January 17, 1964

…Hell week doesn't worry me too much because all I have to do is exist. Actually I'm looking forward to my road trip. During semester break I'll have to do a lot of studying for our [fraternity] lore exam…

May 20, 1964

…Not much is happening except that I got thrown in the shower the other day by a junior and a sophomore. My pledge brothers wouldn't lift a finger to help me. They just stood aside and laughed. Pledge class unity, Ha!

FRATERNITY COOKS

Probably no one is remembered more at the Wabash Beta House than our beloved cook, Jerry Eubank, or "Banks," as we called him. As a student my brother, Steve (Wabash, '63), hired Jerry away from the Crawfordsville County Club. Previously he had the chef at the Jefferson House Smorgasbord in Lafayette.

What I remember most about Jerry was how he was a friend to everyone and a father figure to a few hundred Beta undergraduates over the course of his fifteen-year tenure at the Beta House. Like some bartenders and hairdressers, Jerry was a skilled listener and advice giver to many of us.

As one might imagine, given his resume, Jerry was a great cook. We had many great Sunday dinners and wonderful lunches and dinners on dance weekends. My least favorite of Jerry's dishes was chipped beef on toast, but even that was quite palatable.

Jerry was well known for his Christmas Punch, also known as "Jerry's Eggnog," a recipe which was published by Jerry's brother in *Recipes from Across Indiana*.

Jerry was so beloved by the Betas that he was inducted into the Beta Theta Pi fraternity as an honorary member on December 4, 1976.

FRATERNITY RIVALRIES - NEEDLES & SLEDGEHAMMERS

Rivalries between fraternities at Wabash are legion. These rivalries run the gamut from spirited snowball fights and water fights to which fraternity wins first place at intramural sports, scholarship, homecoming decorations, homecoming queen, and Mother's Day sing.

During my time at Wabash from 1963 to 1967 a rather unique rivalry erupted. During this period the Phi Gams held the editorship of the *Wabash*, our college yearbook. The Phi Gams envied the Betas, who along with the Sigma Chis, had the only two new houses on campus. Perhaps the new Beta house caused the Beta ego to swell a little as they did manage to attract some of the prettiest women to their parties. Perhaps the Betas partied too much as scholarship fell to last place among fraternities during my junior year. Betas also had a reputation for doing very well in intramural sports and captured many first and second place trophies, much to the consternation of the Phi Gams.

At any rate, and whatever the cause, the *Wabash* editors needled the Betas on a yearly basis. Envy ruled and jealousy reigned. The 1964 edition intimated that the Beta intramural squad was more practiced than the college's varsity squads. In the 1965 edition the Betas were knocked for having a new patio and ice machine. The Betas had too many "sports cars." As I recall, one brother did drive his father's powder-blue T-Bird. The crowning blow to the Beta ego came in the 1966 edition in which the Betas were described as "the college jet set" and the "birdmen." The Betas had "nailed down such campus distinctions as having a majority of "Steck's salesmen" Yes, we did dress better than the average Wabash "caveman," or at least the Beta Steck salesman did.

In time, the Betas became fed up with the Phi Gams. One brother, whose name is forever lost in the mists of time, had trouble starting his car, an old jalopy, not the usual "sports car" that we were accused of having. The jalopy could not be repaired so it was emblazoned with quotes from the 1966 *Wabash* and pushed onto the front lawn of the Phi Gam house in the middle of one September night. Not to be outdone, the Phi Gams made much of their new misfortune and sold whacks at the car with a sledgehammer. I can't recall how much a whack cost, but apparently the Phi Gams made enough money to have the car towed away.

FRATERNITY DOGS AT WABASH

Since time immemorial, fraternity house dogs have been a fixture at Wabash College. Now, however, due to liability concerns that isn't the case. The tradition of dogs wandering in and out of class has been lost forever.

When I attended Wabash in the mid-1960s our Beta House mascot was Wooglin, a black and white collie mix. The Lambda Chi's had Khan, a huskie mix, the Delts had George, a boxer, the Phi Delts had Old Ben, a St. Bernard, and the Sigma Chis owned a Great Dane.

A number of dogs around town looked like Wooglin. My wife suspects that we Betas secretly enjoyed Wooglin's exploits and, thus, chose not to have him neutered. Who knows? Recently when I was in Crawfordsville I saw a stray that looked like Woogie. The Beta heritage continues!

Woogie, like other campus dogs, was prone to flatulence. He could empty the Beta TV room quite in an instant. Departing chapter members would whine, "Aw, Woogie," in their haste to exit. We Betas used to have a song with the words, "go to Wooglin when we die." After being around Woogie, I was not sure that I wanted to go there. Wooglin might be an intensely stinky place!

In my last year at Wabash, Jim, one of my pledge brothers, provided a companion for Wooglin. Fritz was a St. Bernard. I felt really sorry for the pledges that had to clean up his drool. One would have to change clothes after one of his dog kisses. Word got to the Phi Delts in Crawfordsville that we should have a "marriage" of the two dogs.

Jim taught Fritz how to speak. From then on Fritz accompanied Jim to required chapel. Whenever the chapel speaker droned on a little too long, Jim would tell Fritz to speak and hopefully end the chapel speech. Sadly, we had to give Fritz away when he went after Dr. Barnes' seeing-eye dog. Alas, Fritz found himself exiled to a farm near Richmond, Indiana.

BROTHER LEE

Lee, one of my Wabash College Beta Theta Pi brothers, was from the South, Texas to be exact. He had a southern drawl and would frequently say, "y'all," instead of "you guys" or "youse guys" if you were from "da Region" as so many of my brothers were. He was a natty dresser, who, as an undergraduate, worked at Steck's, a now defunct Crawfordsville men's clothing emporium. He studied hard and was in top contention for the much coveted "Big Shovel" and "Big Straw" awards that were handed out every year by the Sphinx Club, a group of Wabash elite.

Besides not dressing like a typical Wabash Caveman, Lee behaved a little differently from the rest of us. He used tooth powder instead of toothpaste. He smoked a pipe, a very long pipe. He was a budding Joe O'Rourke, a speech professor. While the rest of us swilled beer, Lee drank J&B scotch from his fraternity mug.

When I was a freshman pledge, Lee was one of those sophomores who did his best to make pledgeship difficult. As pledges we coped with the abuse heaped upon us in a variety of ways. Open rebellion always backfired and even passive aggressiveness was likely to fail. Fighting back in secrecy or under the cover of darkness was our only recourse.

One or two of my pledge brothers paid several visits to Lee's study room. On one visit his Beta mug was glued to his desk. On another talcum powder was substituted for his tooth powder. And on still another visit, pencil shavings were substituted for his pipe tobacco. Such cleverness I had never seen nor could I have ever imagined!

Lee survived our retaliation, graduated, went on to law school, and he became a successful attorney. He has been one of Wabash College's most successful volunteer recruiters of incoming freshmen.

CHAPEL

Chapel has long been a tradition at Wabash College. According to Wabash historian Robert S. Harvey in 1840, religious Chapel attendance was required FOURTEEN times a week. The first Chapel was located in South Hall until it was moved to Center Hall in November 1870. As the student enrollment continued to enlarge, the Chapel in Center Hall was outgrown so Chapel was relocated again to the upper floor of the gymnasium. Beginning in 1920, students were required to attend Chapel every morning except Saturday and Sunday. A number of these Chapel meetings were devoted to music and secular speakers. In 1929 a new addition appeared on the Wabash campus, the now familiar, beautiful brick and wood trim Chapel that greets every freshman on Freshman Sunday. During World War II, Chapel attendance was required only once a week and the Chapel sessions were seldom religious. Beginning in 1946 compulsory Chapel was held on Monday and Thursday mornings. That was the schedule when I attended Wabash. However, beginning in 1970 and extending into 1971 the faculty and students entered into a prolonged heated debate about compulsory Chapel and finally abandoned the practice.

Wabash College Chapel

During my tenure at Wabash with compulsory Chapel twice weekly, we were allowed ten "cuts" per semester. Chapel attendance was strictly enforced by monitors who dutifully registered the attendance of all Wabash students who were required to sit in assigned seats. And woe to the student who exceeded his ten cuts. He was usually asked to stay out of Wabash for at least a semester. I knew of nobody, however, who was kicked out of Wabash for exceeding his ten Chapel cuts. I did have a few Beta brothers who came close to their quota and there was lots of wailing and gnashing of teeth until the semester had ended.

NICKNAMES OF COLLEGE PROFESSORS

It is with some trepidation that I write about the nicknames of some of my favorite Wabash College Division I [Sciences] faculty. Among the student body of the 1960's these nicknames were well known, but the students never ever used these nicknames when personally conversing with a professor. We always used Dr. "so and so" out of the utmost respect.

That said, I must now tell my story about three of my most beloved professors.

Edward Lauth Haenisch, Ph.D., Professor and Chairman of the Chemistry Department, was the designer of the Physics/Chemistry course and author of its accompanying text, which now resides in the Wabash College Archives. This course was a requirement for all students who expected to graduate from Wabash. Physics/Chemistry was dreaded by most non-science majors and caused not a few to spend five years at Wabash. Several students took the course three times in order to graduate.

Dr. Haenisch's nickname was "Heavy Ed." It's a little unclear how he acquired his nickname, but some might suspect it was because he was a bit on the heavy side, but he carried his weight well. Others might suspect he got his nickname because of his booming voice and heavy hand as he smacked a yardstick on the chemistry demonstration table in his attempt to wake up a dozing Division II or III major. One of his favorite expressions was to boom out, "MOLES, MOLES, MOLES." Those who thought that "MOLES" were of the garden variety were sadly mistaken. A mole, or mol, in the language of chemists, is the "quantity of a substance having a weight in grams numerically equal to its molecular weight." (*Webster's New World Dictionary*). Understanding the concept of a mole was essential in performing chemistry calculations. Since I'm not a chemist, let's quickly move on to the next professor.

Eliot Churchill Williams, Ph.D., was a professor in the Biology Department. To the students he was simply known as "E.C." Another favorite nickname was "Bugsy," owing to his keen interest in entomology. Pity the poor student, however, who referred to insects and spiders as "bugs." One of Dr. Williams' research interests was the study of beetles. I understand that he discovered several new species of beetles, which made their home high in the treetops of the Central American rainforest. Dr. Williams was a tall man who cut a handsome figure as he led the academic procession at Wabash graduations for a number of years. He always wore a jaunty-looking hat and carried a fierce looking mace.

Last, but not least, was Robert Ledyard Henry, Ph.D., professor of Physics. Dr. Henry's nickname was "Bullet Bob." An oft-told story of how Dr. Henry acquired his nickname was that one day he was demonstrating the conservation of energy/momentum (Don't ask me to recall the equation! I do know, however, that it involved mass and velocity, however) by firing a .22 caliber rifle into the end of a log which was suspended from the ceiling by two wires. Bob missed the end of the log and the bullet went through the wall into an adjoining Goodrich Hall lecture room. Reportedly no one was injured by his poor marksmanship.

At a reunion some about 20 to 25 years ago, my wife and I were privileged to sit next to Dr. Henry at one of our reunion dinners. Perhaps the alcohol got the better of me, but I screwed up my courage to ask Dr. Henry how he had acquired his nickname. Without affirming or denying the first story, he told us that it may have been the speed with which he threw the softball in student/faculty softball games. Or, he said, it may have been the speed with which he conversed. All three stories make sense, and I'll leave it to the reader to form his or her own conclusions.

WABASH DANCE CHAPERONES

I recently came across article by Mrs. Eliot (Jean) Williams in the *Bachelor,* our college's newspaper ("Faculty Wife Tells All," Vol. LVI, October 5, 1963). This article jogged my memory as I recalled suggesting to our social chairman that we ask Dr. Williams and his wife to chaperone one of the dances at the Beta House.

Dr. Williams was one of my favorite professors at Wabash. I was his lab assistant for a couple of years in Invertebrate Zoology and Ecology. It seemed only natural to suggest to the brothers that we invite Dr. and Mrs. Williams to chaperone our dance. The brothers agreed and they were invited. I recall greeting them during the evening. As the dance ended, my date and I departed the house. The next Monday at our chapter meeting, I was in the proverbial "hot seat." After the dance ended, the Williams "cleaned house." He went to the second and third floor study rooms and routed out any brothers who were still canoodling with their dates. What could I say to the brothers, but that the Williams took their jobs seriously! I was unapologetic. Sad to say, I was never again asked for suggestions about faculty chaperones.

Back to Jean's articles!

In her article, Jean made a tongue in cheek reference to the Betas and the Phi Gams. Searching for titles, she considered "The Night They Turned Out the Lights at the Eta Bit Pi House," "They Thought We Didn't See Them When They Slipped Up to the Dorm," "South Sea Island party: Sarongs and Sex," or "What Were They Really Serving in Those Little Paper Cups?"

Jean went on to describe the uneasy relationship between faculty chaperones and fraternities. Sadly, faculty chaperones were rarely greeted and often totally ignored during dances. At times the senior chaperones did have fun, like dancing to a few tunes of Glenn Miller and Tommy Dorsey. Some of the newer songs and dances proved a bit strenuous for them, however. Remember, "Louie, Louie"?

In 1963 the practice of having chaperones at Wabash dances had not yet been abandoned. As Jean wryly observed, "The Dean of Women at DePauw would hardly let their girls venture into this wolves' den without chaperones."

Finally Jean set out a reasonable series of fourteen tips for social chairmen and twelve tips for chaperones. It appears that in my day as well as the present day, Wabash men still need concrete examples of how to be gentlemen. Where oh where did our mothers and fathers go wrong?

Jean's article became a classic with many requests for reprints from all over the country. It is well worth reading.

THE ALL-CAMPUS WATER FIGHT OF MAY, 1964

"In the Spring a young man's fancy lightly turns to thoughts of love."
Alfred Lord Tennyson, "Locksley Hall" (1842)

Are the words from Tennyson's poem true at Wabash College? Well, not always. Sometimes in the spring at Wabash a young man's fancy turns to water fights. At Wabash, water is much more plentiful than women.

In a May 23, 1964 letter that I wrote my parents, I described the all-campus water fight that had occurred the night before. The Delts and Phi Delts started the melee by attacking the Beta house. Soon the Delts, Phi Psis, and Tekes (then living in the Kane House) had joined the fracas. We threw water balloons, whole wastebaskets full of water. In short we used anything that could hold water. We poured water from the Beta house roof. I recall that one of my Beta brothers started a small fire on the sidewalk leading down from the Beta house. In due time Crawfordsville's finest had arrived with a police car, a fire truck, and a riot vehicle. Of course, our beloved Dean Norman Moore made an appearance. Before long, Dean Moore and several police officers had been doused. The late-night "party" ended with all participants singing "Old Wabash."

Just after we had sung "Old Wabash," someone from the crowd shouted, "Let's go to DePauw." This must have sent a chill up the back of Dean Moore because six years earlier an all-campus water fight had erupted. After it ended, about 125 Wabash men traveled to DePauw. The ensuing water fight at DePauw involved about 1000 students and a number of Wabash men ended up in the Putnam County jail.

WABASH COLLEGE AND CO-EDUCATION

Not many people are aware that the issue of co-education at Wabash College is a very old one, in fact dating to 1861, and a bare 29 years after Wabash was founded. That year Elizabeth Boynton and three of her friends had been granted permission by President Charles White to attend physics lectures given by Professor Campbell at Wabash. Perhaps it was an omen that President White died suddenly of a stroke on October 29, 1861. Then on September 7, 1868 twenty-three young women signed a statement petitioning for admittance. By the 19th of September the faculty and president denied their petition, but sent "their sympathy." Subsequently these women sent the *Crawfordsville Journal* a letter to the editor decrying this decision to "cut away the last hope of receiving an education [whereby depriving] them of their just rights…the faculty of Wabash College 'sympathize' with us but that does not prevent them from closing their doors in our faces…Is this Justice, the remnant of barbarism of the Dark ages of Paganism?…Can the enlightened Faculty of Wabash deliberately weigh in the balance, for their sons, advancement, Christianity, knowledge; and for their daughters narrow-mindedness and ignorance? No, never! The time will come when we will crowd their recitation-rooms [and] literary halls…[ending] the rusty prejudice [of the college with the] college doors slowly and reluctantly opening for us." In a mocking letter to the *Crawfordsville Weekly Journal* on October 22 it was suggested that the women "erect and fit up an extensive kitchen presided over by a competent *professore de cuisine*, in order that the young ladies may be educated for the positions that Heaven designed for them, competent wives, and mothers…"

In 1872 President Joseph Tuttle opined that college would "damage [a woman's] womanly qualities and put her health in serious peril," if they were admitted to Wabash. Over the last thirty years of the nineteenth century the issue of co-education at Wabash surfaced several more times, but each time the issue was voted down by the Board of Trustees, despite Asbury University (now DePauw University) and Indiana University having gone co-ed in 1867.

In the early 1970s, bowing to economic pressures, Wabash College reluctantly agreed to look into the issue of making Wabash College co-educational. The SCADEW committee (Study Committee on the Advantages and Disadvantages of Educating Women at Wabash) was formed to study the issue. The committee issued their report on September 22, 1972. Although a substantial minority of faculty and students were in favor of co-education, the Board of Trustees was not, and they subsequently bowed to the pressure of ancient alums who threatened to discontinue their donations to Wabash if it became educational. One wonders if the name of the SCADEW committee wasn't short for "23 skidoo," denoting a fervent wish that the issue would quickly disappear into thin air.

An interesting side-light to the issue of co-education at Wabash is that in 1973 a woman, Terri Lee Meade, applied for admission to Wabash. She sought help from Indiana Senators Hartke and Bayh and the ACLU, but all for naught, because the Board of Trustees voted unanimously to deny her admission.

The co-education issue erupted again in the late 1980s and early 1990s, perhaps as a result of the heightened interest in women's issues during that time period. This time the faculty was strongly behind making Wabash co-educational so as to better educate men in how to deal with women in our modern working world. Some 67 Wabash faculty members, including some of Wabash most prestigious professors, were in favor of Wabash going co-educational. However, there was a strong minority of equally prestigious Wabash professors who were against co-education. But again the Board of Trustees refused to budge. In fact, the co-educational issue had become so fractious that President Frank Sheldon Wettack resigned after only four years in office.

The issue of co-education at Wabash College has not surfaced in the past 20 years. I suspect that this is so because no Wabash College president since President Wettack has wanted to serve a shortened tenure. Apparently "the time [hasn't yet] come when [women] will crowd [Wabash's] recitation-rooms." In 2013, Wabash faculty women and visiting women guests finally have adequate restroom facilities on campus.

FUN IN CRAWFORDSVILLE

Amanda, my physical therapist, a recent graduate of Franklin College and the University of Indianapolis, recently asked me what we did for fun in Crawfordsville when I attended Wabash. I was at a loss for words, since on weekends we usually left Crawfordsville in our quest for women at other Indiana colleges and universities. We left by any conveyance possible, car, bus, even by canoe down Sugar Creek. As I rapidly searched my memory banks for an answer to Amanda's question, I uttered, "Well...um...er..." Finally I blurted out, "We shot rats at the Crawfordsville dump! I even took a date there once!" Then my memory of springtime water fights sprang to mind. We had campus dances. We painted the senior bench.

Since my original conversation with Amanda, I have looked at pictures from the Beta Theta Pi archives. Looking at these pictures enabled me to come up with some other "fun" things that we did at Wabash.

I found a picture of brother Jim who collected bets on whether he could do 1000 sit-ups. I was uncertain of the number at first, but pledge brothers, Clark and Haines are in agreement that it was indeed 1000. Clark also recalled that once Jim took bets on how many hard-boiled eggs that he could eat in one sitting.

I also dug up a photo of Beta brothers in the basement watching "movies." The gentle reader should note that these weren't ordinary movies. It seems that an entrepreneurial student from another Indiana college would make the rounds of Wabash fraternities and living units, collect a small fee from each individual, and then show 1920s era movies which were without sound. We provided our own sound with plenty of whoops and yells. I can even remember the plot of one of the movies, but that is another story.

Lest anyone consider the Betas typical "Wabash Cavemen," one photo features another brother Jim at the piano before a "typical"

Beta evening dinner. He was an accomplished pianist in those days, in contrast to his later image as a "hoorah" USAF F-111 attack pilot.

I also recall that we watched a little TV in our rec room. Football was always of great interest to us and we, of course, were glued to the TV screen during the first Super Bowl championship in 1967.

The Beatles were extremely popular at the time and at least three of my pledge-brothers brought their record players when they moved into the Beta house. Most of the brothers were present to watch the Beatles on the Ed Sullivan show in 1964 and 1965. And who can forget John Kennedy's assassination in November, 1963? The mood was quite somber that day in the Beta TV room. This was not fun.

CANOEING DOWN SUGAR CREEK

A time-honored tradition at Wabash is a canoe trip down Sugar Creek, which extends through Montgomery and Parke Counties of Indiana before it empties into the Wabash River. Sugar Creek flows through two Indiana State Parks, the Shades and Turkey Run. It is quite scenic and is the fastest flowing waterway in Indiana, so it's very popular with canoeists.

In May of one year while I was at Wabash College I decided to make a personal foray down Sugar Creek. Although I hardly mentioned the trip to my parents, it was quite memorable. My pledge brother Jim and I borrowed my grandmother's car and left it at Turkey Run State Park, twenty-three miles from Crawfordsville. We hitchhiked back to Crawfordsville where we rented a canoe and started on our big adventure. It was warm and sunny that day. The creek was running fast due to recent rains. We packed a picnic lunch. All went well, until about two thirds of the way through our journey. We took the wrong fork around an island and got hung up on a rock. We finally dislodged ourselves, but the canoe filled with water and I lost my paddle. We finally were able to beach and drain the canoe and were on our way again, but with only one paddle. We were still quite wet and beginning to feel a little chilly, as it was late afternoon. Finally we arrived at the footbridge, which crosses over Sugar Creek at Turkey Run State Park. We loaded up our canoe and returned to Crawfordsville. We were exhausted but certainly had a thrilling day while experiencing the wilds of Indiana from our canoe on Sugar Creek.

PANTY RAID AT DEPAUW UNIVERSITY

Panty raids are legend at coed colleges and universities. My parents had regaled me with stories about panty raids when they attended DePauw and Indiana Universities. The problem was that I attended an all-male college, not a coed in sight. What to do? It didn't take me long to decide that I should stage a raid at DePauw University. I collected three other pledge brothers and we were off in one of their cars. We attacked Rector Hall, an all-female dorm of mostly freshman women. However, our loud shouts for panties failed to attract much attention and no panties emerged from the windows. We decided to enter the dorm and raced upstairs. Still no reaction, so two of us raced back downstairs and then upstairs again. By the time we arrived upstairs the second time, some women had pushed a bed out into the hall to block us. I jumped on the bed and received a horrified look from one of the residents. Still no panties were thrown to reward us. We raced downstairs and out but not before our two other compatriots had created some mischief in the basement.

After we came downstairs the second time, we were privileged to meet the supervisor of Rector Hall. Two of my brothers had turned on the fire hose in the basement, not very hard, mind you, but hard enough to slightly dampen the floor. The dean at DePauw called our Dean Moore the following day. We culprits were invited in to talk to Dean Moore, and, although he seemed slightly amused at the incident, admonished us not to do it again.

PALM SUNDAY TORNADO IN MONTGOMERY COUNTY

With the coming of each tornado season, my mind always goes back to the Palm Sunday tornado outbreak of April 11, 1965. Early in the evening some of us at the Wabash College Beta house watched the ominous greenish-grey mammatus cloud formations roll overhead. Later we learned that an F4 twister had struck along Indiana 32 between Shannondale and Dover.

This particular tornado started on the southeast side of Crawfordsville and traveled nearly 50 miles through Montgomery, Boone, and Hamilton counties. It caused 28 deaths, 100 injuries, and destroyed over 80 homes.

Overall this Midwestern tornado outbreak was the second largest on record; it included 78 tornadoes, killed 271 people, and injured 1500. This tornado outbreak was the third deadliest on record, trailing the Super Outbreak (148 tornadoes in 13 states) of 1974 which killed 315 and the Tri-State Tornado (Missouri, Illinois, and Indiana) of 1925 which took 747 lives.

Back in 1965 Wabash College didn't offer immersion trips to help clean-up and rebuild after weather-related disasters. However, we Wabash men pitched in to help with the clean-up. Two days after the tornado approximately 40 Wabash men gathered at the Shannondale Presbyterian Church to receive their work assignments.

The following day about 100 students pitched in to clean up debris. I was a part of this latter contingent and I remember the disbelief and horror I felt when I glimpsed the utter destruction of a number of farm houses and barns.

All that was left of some structures were splinters of wood two or three feet long and several inches wide. Some woods were simply blown down. In other places, large trees were snapped off at their mid-sections.

We piled the debris in large piles which were to be burned later by the farmers. We worked quietly. I think we were far too shaken by the sight of such destruction to be able to talk much, much less crack a few jokes.

I'm glad I joined the clean-up. Forty-five years later, the raw power of Mother Nature is still indelibly impressed upon my memory.

CHAPTER 5

DATING AND MARRIAGE

"I stole my first kiss by chasing a little girl around my first grade classroom just after lunchtime."

KISSES ENSHRINED IN TIME, OR KISS AND TELL

I stole my first kiss by chasing a little girl around my first grade classroom just after lunchtime. My mother had told me that she and this girl's mother had been college friends. What was I thinking? If this had happened today, I would have been expelled.

While I was in high school, to ensure a long goodnight kiss, I enlisted the aid of a girlfriend's brother and his male friend. They hoisted me upon their shoulders and I unscrewed the light bulb above the back steps to my girlfriend's home. We called ourselves "the tripod." Later that night, as my girlfriend and I kissed, I could hear her mother just inside the door feverishly switching the light on and off while mumbling under her breath about why the light wouldn't work.

I learned the hard way not to date two young women at the same time when they live in close proximity to one other. Once I dated two young ladies at the same time and I heard through the grapevine that a third young lady had been a go-between. By the next morning after a date with one, the other was in full possession of all of the details of the previous night's date with the other. The kisses might have been sweeter had it not been for that third young woman. You live and learn!

I wasn't fast, or so I thought. I'd date a girl three times before trying for a goodnight kiss. This didn't work with a Biblical fundamentalist. Not only were my advances rejected but she spread a rumor that I "was fast." I secretly enjoyed my newfound reputation!

"How tall are you," I said. "I'm four feet ten inches," one girlfriend said proudly. With alacrity, she leapt to the edge of her parent's couch and gave me a sensuously long kiss before I left for the evening. I was delighted and thought she was quite ingenious in both her moves and kissing ability.

Once I dated a young woman from out-of-town. My father had loaned me his T-Bird which had a huge center console with bucket seats on either side. Somehow I managed to maneuver my torso on her side of the car. She pressed herself against me for a long and sensuous kiss. I must have been totally flummoxed because I scraped my rear fender against a stone wall as I exited her driveway after escorting her to her door.

I took another young woman to our local drive-in movie theater. *War Wagon* with John Wayne was playing. Somehow we managed to steam up the windows and missed most of the show. I guess drive-ins really are passion pits! Years later I watched *War Wagon* on video to see what I had missed. It was a pretty good movie, but the kissing was better!

She was short, "five-two," she said. She needed to stand on her back stoop to reach my lips comfortably. Her kisses were intoxicating. When we kissed on a steep hillside in Butler University's Holcomb Gardens, the love chemicals coursing through our veins were so dizzyingly powerful that we almost fell over and rolled down the hill.

My mother said, "Kisses lead to things," and I guess they do. I married the last woman I dated and kissed. We lingered a little too long over our kiss after the minister had pronounced us husband and wife. Our kiss was interrupted by the pastor's all-too audible "a-hem."

DATING AT WABASH

At Wabash dating is a time-honored tradition. Since Wabash is an all-male college, men travel to get dates at nearby colleges and universities such as DePauw, Butler, Purdue, Indiana, Saint Mary of the Woods, Indiana State, and Ball State. During the week Wabash students knuckle down and study hard and on weekends they play hard.

The following excerpts from letters home to my parents describe my dating experiences during my first two years at Wabash. As a more mature adult, I now look back and see how utterly naive I was. I was alternately high or low depending upon how my date life was progressing. When I didn't have a steady girlfriend, I rationalized by feeling sorry for the brothers who did have a steady dating relationship.

November 20, 1963

...I really enjoyed my date last weekend and was planning to have another date with her until I received her thank-you note. It says, "Though I hate to admit it to you, I certainly think that the DePauw men out-class yours. Can't put my finger on it exactly..." We (the other boys I showed the letter to and myself) all had a good laugh over it. How green can a girl get? If that's the typical DePauw girl, I don't want any part of it. I'm letting myself cool off before I write a reply or I might be tempted to make a few really caustic remarks. Even so, it's going to be a cold letter. Maybe she'll realize her mistake and apologize...

February 20, 1964

...The weekend after this is [Miami] Triad. Haines fixed me up with an Alpha Chi pledge from DPU [DePauw University]. I got a letter from her today. She sounds very clever. I wish you could read it...

April 9, 1964

...I'm going down to DPU this weekend for the Little 500. The girl from Evansville, who I had up for the last house dance, invited me. She even sent me a favor to her last dance even though we were there only thirty minutes. Playing the field really pays off and I have no intentions of stopping. By the way, Haines got pinned last night. The poor guy has to go down there every weekend and sometimes in the middle of the week...

April 15, 1964

...My date Friday night didn't turn out so well after all. [She] likes me but I don't like her. She can't talk. That has happened twice before. On the other hand, I liked [another young woman], but she didn't care for me. Maybe someday I'll meet a girl that I like, who likes me. Meanwhile I couldn't be less concerned...

Friday, October 9 [1964]

...I'm going to see Kathy at DePauw Sunday. Perhaps I'll run into Nell. Anyway, I'm planning to see her sometime before long...

Friday, [December 13, 1964]

...[My date] is coming up for a dance this weekend. Don't worry. We plan to do a lot of studying...

Monday [January 4, 1964]

[A DePauw student] has asked me to the Gold-Diggers' Ball this Saturday.

April 17, 1965

...Changing the subject, I had a date with Nell last night. I've never met such a real lady. She has a tremendous sense of humor. I invited her to Pan-Hel and she accepted enthusiastically even before she knew the date, which is, by the way, May 7 and 8. I hope you, Dad, weren't planning to stay Friday night after the bank meeting. No offense, of course, but...

"Dating at Wabash" first appeared in my book, *In their own Words: Hoosier ancestor and family journeys* (Bloomington, Indiana: iUniverse, 2009)

COMPUTER-MATCHED DATES DANCE AT WABASH

When I entered Wabash as a freshman in the fall of 1963 we had a notable lack of computers. This lack was rectified sometime in the next year when an IBM 1620 computer arrived and was lodged in the bowels of the newly-built Baxter Hall. Before long, some genius, a math major no doubt, got the bright idea of obtaining dates via computer matching.

A suitable 38-question, multiple-choice questionnaire was designed. Questions ranged from those about background to qualities desired in a date, such as religion, racial preference, and height. I dutifully filled out this questionnaire along with 88 other date-hungry Wabash men. Our results were reduced to punches on an IBM card and were fed into the computer.

The results spit out of the computer and "Voila!" we were suitably matched with one of 43 women from Western College for Women in Oxford, Ohio and 45 women from St. Mary-of-the-Woods College in Terre Haute, Indiana.

The women all arrived by bus on a beautiful afternoon in October 1965. Their arrival was punctuated by chaos as the number of Wabash who students showed up exceeded the number of arriving women. In my day we called these guys "bird dogs." They pointed, swooped in, and pounced on their intended prey. The cads! I was lucky, however, and obtained the number of my date, found her, and enjoyed lunch at the Campus Center. After lunch, my charming date from St. Mary's and I enjoyed the Hanover vs. Wabash football game. Later I introduced her to my grandmother, who was putting her up for the night at her home just south of Crawfordsville. That evening we enjoyed music by the Primates, a home-grown Wabash band, in the old gymnasium. All in all, this junior Wabash student had a very enjoyable weekend with a classy senior from St. Mary's.

Do any of today's students even know what an IBM card looks like? And what about "hanging chads"? Horrors! A "Caveman" might have gone on and mistakenly married the wrong woman due to the negligence of the infernal IBM computer.

This selection was written for the website *Wabash Stories*, the brainchild of Bruce Gras, (Wabash, '68).

SEPARATION AND DIVORCE

Living on the same street
Preadolescents we met.
Uncertain of our bodies and ourselves,
We separate.

Reunited again,
We're going to the same high school and
Each wanting to become doctors.
Will our dreams be fulfilled?

Reunited again,
And living on the same island,
We have our first date, then my family moves away.
We separate, and I leave feeling sad and empty.

Separated by miles and miles,
We have our second date,
Then John F. Kennedy dies.
We separate again.

Reunited again,
And separated by only 30 miles,
Some more dates.
"Why don't you get married," her sister said and we said, "OK."

Martin Luther King, Jr. dies,
Robert F. Kennedy dies,
And we weep.
Years pass.

Our love dies.
We're too different to stay together.
There's divorce and unbearable pain,
But then rebirth.

WEDDING DAY

Liz and I became engaged in November, 1980. We picked out her wedding ring on Valentine's Day, 1981 and spent the summer of 1981 planning our wedding with Liz doing most of the work while consulting regularly with me. Her mother had died on New Year's Eve 1980, so she did not have any mother-of-the-bride advice. With the exception of $300 that her mother had given her toward her eventual wedding, she financed everything from her second-year resident salary. Her mother's gift bought her wedding gown.

My father was kind enough to provide our rehearsal dinner the night before the wedding at the Iron Skillet Restaurant in Indianapolis. I felt badly about telling my Dad that he couldn't serve liquor, not even wine, at the dinner, but Liz's Dad was a teetotaler and had strong religious compunctions against drinking and we did not want to deeply offend him. I was quite certain however, that Dad had a traveling flask hidden somewhere, probably in the car, and took a short snort prior to dinner. I'll bet Mother had one too.

Our wedding day September 5, 1981 dawned warm and humid and kept getting hotter and hotter. Early that morning we finished moving Liz's possessions from her west-side apartment to my home on Graceland Avenue where her father had spent the night.

I have no idea what I ate for breakfast or lunch that day. What I do recall is that we arrived at church in plenty of time, probably around noon, and proceeded to get dressed for the 1:30 P.M. ceremony. Before too long Liz came to me in a panic. "I have to have my hoop," she said. I naively said, "What hoop?" "The hoop for my dress," Liz replied. Lacking any knowledge of wedding dresses and thinking that hoops under skirts went out of style in the late nineteenth century, I asked, "Are you sure you need it?" She assured me she did, so I embarked on a cross-town trip to retrieve her hoop and preserve our future marital harmony. I arrived back at Tabernacle Presbyterian Church, hot and sweaty and a little perturbed, but with that hoop slip in hand. It was my introduction to married life with Liz and finding her lost items.

Any frustration that I had quickly evaporated when Liz appeared at the far end of the sanctuary and slowly strolled down the aisle on the arm of her father, proceeding to the lovely strains of Bach's *Jesu, Joy of Man's Desiring.*" Did she pick that processional out on purpose? This man was quite "desirous" at that particular moment. She looked so lovely in her wedding gown, hoop included.

I observed a bobble at the far end of the isle as Liz's father stepped on her wedding dress, causing her to stumble slightly. Regaining her composure, Liz proceeded down the aisle with more space between her and her father. As her father released her I noticed that her hands were trembling. I relieved any last minute worries that she might have had by gently holding her hands in mine and patting them.

Liz felt it was not appropriate for a 27-year-old woman who chose her own mate to be "given away" by her father, like a sack of flour being passed from Dad to husband. Instead, she spoke to her father about how he had taught her the true meaning of marriage vows by his faithfulness to her mother during their long marriage and the care he rendered during her mother's long terminal illness from breast cancer. Then she asked his blessing on our marriage. Through tears, he gave it. Liz says the only other times she'd seen her father cry was when his mother and his wife had died. I was later told that by this time, there was hardly a dry eye in the church; even Pastor Hunter's voice was choked up when he next tried to speak. Vows said, it came time for the wedding kiss. We lingered a bit too long, however, and our minister gave a not too subtle clearing of his throat which brought that kiss to a screeching halt.

We then preceded arm in arm back down the aisle to Beethoven's *Ode to Joy.* I was joyfully walking a bit too fast and Liz had to hold me back to slow me down. I was just stepping lively to the music! She later told me the photographer was signaling us to slow down so he could get pictures of us in the aisle. Really, I wasn't trying to hot-foot it out of there!

Our wedding photo

Our wedding reception was held in the church parlor, again with no alcohol. Liz's maid of honor, Kimra, and bridesmaids (Karen, Dawn, and Betsy) had kindly prepared a sumptuous variety of delicious home-made *hors d'oeuvres* and orange sherbet punch. The only reception food purchased was the wedding cake. We froze the top layer of the cake and gobbled it down on our first anniversary as I recall.

After the reception we were ready to take off, or so I thought. Ed, my best man, had hidden the slacks which I had planned to wear. After much begging and pleading, I finally got my slacks back and we proceeded to our car, which had been highly decorated in the usual fashion!

After carrying Liz across the threshold of our house, one of my first tasks was to wash our car which we planned to take on our honeymoon. We opened our wedding gifts in our family room and finally we were off mid-evening to dinner at *La Tour*, an up-scale downtown French restaurant on the top floor of the Indiana National Bank. We had delicious pheasant *en croute*. We were alone, so we each enjoyed a glass of wine.

Our first night as a married couple was surreptitiously spent in our home. We hid our car in the garage, kept the lights low, and the curtains drawn so as not to alert the neighbors who would have gladly joined our best man and the wedding party to provide a midnight *Charivari*, had they known we were home. Our best man was completely surprised and chagrined when he later learned we were at home rather than in a Cincinnati or Kentucky hotel that night. He was ready for a 2 A.M. bell-ringing.

The next day we were off on our honeymoon which we planned to spend in the Smokey Mountains and on the Blue Ridge Parkway. We stayed at Gatlinburg a couple of nights and I'll never forget the look on Liz's face when she saw all those shops. She had the uncanny ability to stand at the threshold of a shop, calmly survey the interior, and then decide if the shop was worthy of further inspection. Boy, did I have a lot to learn!

We took in lovely Asheville, North Carolina and surrounding areas, with Appalachian crafts and endless mountains fading into the distance. It was a wonderful week of travel and time together that began what has been a long and very loving marriage. Each of us says we'd marry the other again in a heartbeat, but maybe without the hoop skirt slip next time!

CHAPTER 6

MEDICAL SCHOOL, INTERNSHIP, AND RESIDENCY

"You want this next suture cut too short or too long?"

MEDICAL SCHOOL

I attended Indiana University School of Medicine in Indianapolis and graduated with my MD degree in 1971. I can well recall my medical school interview which was held in Bloomington, Indiana. One of my first questions was, "Where did you park?" I sheepishly answered, "On a very faded yellow curb line. I hope it's legal." Fortunately my car, sans parking ticket, was still there when I returned. Unfortunately parking is still a problem at IU in Bloomington. Another question was, "Where did you get your sports coat…Stecks?" "Matter of fact, I did," I answered. Stecks was a men's clothing store in Crawfordsville. I was rather put off by one of the three interviewers who kept his head in a newspaper during the entire interview. I thought it best to keep my feelings to myself that this behavior was highly inappropriate. A third question was, "What about this C in second semester organic chemistry? Did you have a personality conflict with your professor?" I thought to myself, "Did they know my professor?" but I quietly said "No, it was a tough course." This had been my only C grade at Wabash and only one quarter of the students who had started the course finished it.

I was used to small class sizes at Wabash, so being in a lecture hall with over two hundred other students, most of whom had been in the top ten percent of their college graduating class, was quite an adjustment. There was no individual attention to be had if you were floundering; only a painful trip to the Student Promotions Committee if all did not go well. Fortunately, that was a trip I avoided.

Another big adjustment at IU Med School was the incredible amount of material that had to be ingested and regurgitated during the first year and a half of basic science courses. It was study, study, study, all the time. There was no time for socialization, much to the chagrin of my new wife. Studying hard did pay off because I made a solid B average during my preclinical studies. It was a real relief when our class finally began the second semester of the second year and began to learn about real diseases in our course called "An Introduction to Medicine."

One of my more interesting courses during my first two years was a special course in human sexuality. Despite its not being an official course, I remember Emerson Hall (our large lecture hall) being packed with standing room only on the evenings that it met. Masters and Johnson's foundational work, *Human Sexual Response* had just been published in 1966, so interest was high, not that it wouldn't have been anyway! Teaching videotapes were rare at that time, so our professors had to improvise and use what some would consider unconventional… porno films. I can still remember students peeling out of the parking lot in the evenings after these sessions. I guessed they were in a rush to get home and demonstrate their new-found knowledge to their spouses.

Oh, the stories that I could tell about medical school! I'll skip some of them in deference to the sensibilities of my gentle readers. I'll include a few, however, some of which I heard second or third hand.

Many stories involve general surgery and the surgical sub-disciplines. One classmate was cutting sutures for a well-known Indianapolis surgeon. He was repeatedly told that he had cut the sutures either too short or two long. He finally asked in frustration, "You want this next suture cut too short or too long?" The same surgeon became exasperated during another surgical case, broke sterile field, went to the window, opened it, and yelled out, "Can anybody help me here, because no one in this operating room can." Another story occurred in an OB-Gyn outpatient clinic. When the intern trying to cauterize a lesion on a woman's cervix accidently brushed her pubic hair with the cauterizing tool, it caught on fire. The flash fire didn't burn the woman, but it was a source of embarrassment for both and a source of amusement to some in that department.

My most embarrassingly painful story occurred during my second year when I was learning to take a history and do a physical exam. I was assigned a patient in the "bullpen," a large 16-patient one-room men's ward at our local Veteran's Administration Hospital. Visual privacy was only afforded by curtains which completely encircled each patient's bed.

I was new at the history taking business and was very compulsive. I read questions from a "cheat-sheet" that I had written so I would not miss anything. My patient that afternoon was extremely hard of hearing, so I had to shout my questions. So much for any semblance of privacy! As I compulsively went down my list of questions for the review of systems, I shouted, "Are you hard of hearing." There was a sickening brief silence and then all the men in the entire bullpen erupted in raucous laughter. Boy was I embarrassed!

My first clinical rotation was on neurology; a good place to get my feet wet and apply my knowledge of electrolyte balance while administering intravenous fluids. Jeff, one of my neurology peers, lost a stroke patient one night, but was given accolades the next morning by the neurology resident who said, "Well, at least he died in perfect electrolyte balance." Such is the dark humor of medical wards. I had my medicine and surgery junior year clerkships at the VA hospital, a good place to learn both subjects, but unfortunately I had no female patients during those six months. I recall one patient I had on medicine who unfortunately had developed colon cancer. Because of my interest in him, I scrubbed in at his surgery after he had been transferred to the surgery service. Much to the annoyance of my peers on surgery, I was treated like royalty in the surgical suite and asked to stand on a stool and feel around in this gentleman's open abdomen. Unlike me, my surgical peers on their surgical rotation were stuck with holding retractors and were berated for their lack of interest in surgery. My pediatrics rotation was a bummer because I was based at Riley Hospital, a tertiary care pediatric facility, and all I got to see were zebras (rare diseases).

During my junior year, I had my psychiatry rotation at Midtown Community Mental Health Center at Marion County General Hospital. I saw a wide variety of patients and it was there that I decided to go into psychiatry. One patient in particular cemented my desire to enter psychiatry. He was a freshman college student just arrived from the Orient. After a semester he decided he did not want to continue in his chosen major and decided to hang himself, since he felt he had been a failure and suicide was his only honorable option. He was so depressed that he had severe psychomotor retardation, an inability to talk or move much. I started him on a tricyclic antidepressant and watched as he slowly emerged from his depression. When he was finally able to speak, we talked about college and I suggested that he change majors, a common occurrence among most American college students. He readily accepted this idea and was discharged to resume his college career. This encounter impressed me with the power of both medication and psychotherapy in treating depression.

As a senior I took a number of electives, mostly away from the IU Medical Center, so that I could see a wider variety of more common illnesses. My electives included Ob-Gyn, pathology, psychiatry, medicine, dermatology and orthopedics. My preceptors in the non-psychiatric disciplines were more than happy to share with me the psychiatric problems associated with their particular specialty. A psychiatric elective at the Purdue Student Health Center made me certain that psychiatry was the career that I wanted to pursue.

INTERNSHIP

Although I could have gone straight into a three-year psychiatry residency after medical school, I chose not to do so. These residencies were available for a short time, but before long the American Board of Psychiatry and Neurology saw their error and reinstated a requirement for an internship of sorts. The first year of this reinstituted four-year residency of psychiatry would contain at least six months of medicine and neurology.

I chose a rotating internship at Methodist Hospital in Indianapolis because I wanted to practice as a "real physician" before I started my psychiatry residency. As a rotating intern we had considerable leeway in choosing services. It was expected, however that we would spend at least two or three months staffing the emergency room (ER). I loved working in the ER. We rotated among the morning, afternoon and night shifts. I saw things that I hadn't seen in medical school including acute trauma, all of the childhood diseases, kidney stones, goiters, strokes, acute heart attacks, etc. Of course, we saw the frequent flyers, folks who were in and out of the ER on almost a daily basis, and whole families with dripping noses because they were too poor to have a family physician. I learned how to suture in the ER and did a whole lot of it. I liked the ER so much that I elected to take more of it.

During my internship I took two months of inpatient psychiatry to see what private practice was all about. I saw my first patient with borderline personality disorder (BPD) there, although BPD would not become a diagnosis until 1980. She was a self-cutter who we sent to the ER to be sutured on a regular basis. One ER doc got so exasperated with her that he sutured her up without injecting Zylocaine. She had the last laugh, however, because she felt nothing. She's learned to dissociate her physical sensations, something that probably never occurred in the mind of the ER physician.

I took two months of outpatient neurology, which fortunately fulfilled my neurology requirement in my psychiatry residency. During my neurology rotation I saw a variety of common neurological problems including migraine headaches, seizure disorders, transient ischemic attacks (TIAs), multiple sclerosis, movement disorders, myasthenia gravis, and peripheral neuropathies.

I also took a couple of months of inpatient internal medicine. It was here that I saw some heartbreaking cases, one of which I will never forget. He was a middle-aged male who was depressed and had abdominal pain, weight loss, and nausea and vomiting. We were certain that he had pancreatic cancer, but there was no way to prove it at the time since our tests just weren't specific enough. In pouring through his chart, I noted that he had a possible midline-mass on his chest x-ray. Further x-rays confirmed this and he was sent for a bronchoscopy. He died of a burst blood vessel during the biopsy. Should we have left well enough alone and not pursued a firmer diagnosis and left him to die an uncomfortable death from pancreatic cancer? To this day I cannot answer that question.

As during junior clerkships, night call was expected of interns. We pulled night call every fourth or fifth night. There was no time off the next day, so we often worked 36 hours with little sleep. We made life and death decisions while on night call, but more about that later.

My year at Methodist Hospital was strenuous, but I would trade it for nothing. It gave me the chance to put it all together as a physician and prepare for what was to come during my psychiatry residency. It gave me experiences that I have never had again, and knowledge I've called on many times with physically ill psychiatric patients.

PSYCHIATRY RESIDENCY

I completed my residency in psychiatry at Indiana University Hospitals at the Indiana University Medical Center (IUMC) in Indianapolis. IUMC has always been diverse and still is. It contains University Hospital, the Richard Roudebush Veterans' Administration Hospital, Riley Hospital for Children, Larue D. Carter Memorial Hospital (for psychiatric patients), and Marion County General Hospital (now Wishard Hospital and soon to be Eskenazi Health System). As residents we were expected to cover all these hospitals at night, a formidable task.

My residency consisted of six-month rotations on both the male and female unisex psychiatry services at Carter Hospital, a six-month rotation in the Riley Hospital Child Psychiatry Clinic, 15 months (nine months of which were elective) in the now defunct Long Hospital Adult Psychiatry Clinic, and three months at Midtown Community Mental Health Center housed at General Hospital. I also consulted for 15 months at the Plainfield, Indiana Reception Diagnostic Center (RDC) for first-time male felons. During our residency training we were expected to follow patients in long-term psychodynamic psychotherapy for two years and these patients might come from any of the aforementioned facilities. We residents ran a journal club for psychiatric literature discussion and were expected to attend Psychiatry Grand Rounds which met on a weekly basis, except during the summer.

I had a lot of wonderful supervisors and mentors during my residency training. These included Drs. Patricia Sharpley, Helio Perez, Don Moore, Frank Walker, Iver and Joyce Small, and Bill Fisher. There were others and I don't mean to slight them. Their stories are recounted in *Psychiatry in Indiana: The First 150 Years* (Bloomington, Indiana: iUniverse, 2010), so I won't repeat them here.

I have many stories about my time in residency training, some repeatable and some not, but here are a few that I can relate:

I had a male patient at Carter Hospital who would smoke cigarette butts that he had scavenged from various ash trays about the admission ward. This was an unusual habit that I hoped to eradicate. Try as I might, nothing seemed to work until I came across the work of Milton Erickson, a brilliant psychiatrist noted for his work in hypnosis and paradoxical intention. So one day I gathered some cigarette butts from an ashtray and invited this young man into an interview room. I proceeded to choose a cigarette butt, put it to my lips, lit it, and took a puff. My patient looked startled and said, "Oh, you smoke cigarette butts too." At that point I was really worried that I might have just reinforced his obnoxious habit. I offered him a cigarette butt, and, as luck would have it, he proceeded to say, "You don't really want me to smoke these, do you?" I answered, "That's right, I don't." Sweet success!

During my year in inpatient psychiatry at Carter Hospital we had what was called weekly admission conferences. As I look back on these conferences I am horrified that we were expected to participate because everyone on the three or four treatment teams was expected to attend and these included the psychiatry resident, his or her staff psychiatrist, the social worker, medical students, occupational and recreational therapists, the hospital chaplain, and various other students. Our large interview room was full of people. To this mix was added two or three patients per week who were paraded in separately to be interviewed by different psychiatry residents. I had no problem with team meetings where the patient met with the treatment team, but the admission conferences with so many people not associated with the treatment team seemed cruel and exhibitionistic.

Night call provided a valuable experience. It was exhausting as well, since we covered very busy emergency rooms at General Hospital and the VA Hospital. It was there that we saw many acutely ill suicidal and psychotic patients. It was our job to evaluate and admit them to the hospital. I remember one patient, a malingerer, who worked his way down the line of hospitals on West Tenth Street from west to east. I saw him first at the VA Hospital. When I wouldn't admit him there, he showed up at Carter Hospital. When I refused to admit him there, he said in an exasperated tone, "Well, I'm going to General Hospital next," to which I replied, "I guess I'll see you there." Fortunately he got the message and did not show up.

When I rotated through Midtown we sometimes conducted home visits. Once we were asked to visit a young man with schizophrenia who had been known to be violent in the past. However, he locked himself in his room when we arrived and refused to come out. We promptly left after telling his mother that it was safer to call the police.

At the RDC I evaluated prisoners with mental health problems. The first time I went through security at RDC and heard the heavy mental gates clang shut behind me, it was an eerie feeling. To maintain our safety we interviewed prisoners in front of the guards who were enclosed behind glass partitions. They could come to our aid if need be. Fortunately I never needed their assistance. During my entire time there I never met a prisoner who took responsibility for his crime. It was always "someone else's fault."

A Riley I saw child outpatients and their families. I vividly recall seeing a six or seven year old girl who had been sexually abused. I thought that I could get her to talk about her experience by arranging a doll house with all of the pertinent furniture and doll figures. Was I mistaken! She took one look at the set-up and hurriedly went to play with other toys. I learned an important lesson in play therapy. Things can't be rushed. You have to wait for the lead of the child and engage them where they are.

I recall one particularly hairy session in boys activity therapy at Riley. Jim, my co-therapist supervisor, was gone that day, so I was all alone with six or seven unruly preadolescent boys. I thought maybe I could engage them in a quiet activity of building models. When I opened the door to the supply closet, they carried off as many models as their little arms could carry. We did all make it to our group room, but then one young man proceeded to open the screenless window, straddle the windowsill, and threaten to jump from the third floor. Fortunately I was able to coax him back in, but I was a nervous wreck.

I loved doing long-term psychodynamic psychotherapy so I took a none-month elective at the Long Adult Psychiatry Clinic. There I got training in both group psychotherapy and hypnosis, which each proved valuable in my career.

We residents had a lot of fun together in our off time. I recall participating in a watermelon seed spitting contest in the middle of historic Zionsville. We went caving in southern Indiana. After getting ourselves thoroughly muddy, we would then go to the quarries around Bloomington and swim to wash ourselves off. Some even went skinny-dipping.

Fortunately I didn't have any patients who committed suicide during my residency. I'm not aware of any of my patients killing anybody either. All in all, psychiatry training was an extremely valuable experience for which I've had life-long gratitude.

DEATH AND DYING

By the time I got to medical school I was no stranger to death and dying since I had already lost two grandparents and a third died the summer after my freshman year.

Neither my brother nor I had known our Grandfather Merle Coons as he had died in 1940, a year before Steve was born. The next to go was my grandfather Frank Richman who died when I was almost 11 in 1956. He had a lingering illness due to colon cancer and had undergone a colostomy. I remember us taking several Thanksgiving Day hikes in Marott Park, just north of our home in Sherwood Village. It was so much fun to get out in the cool crisp fall air and hike up and down the hills in Marott Park with the dead leaves rustling beneath our footsteps. Sometime before he died Steve and I were ushered into his bedroom on 53rd Street in Indianapolis and he showed us his colostomy bag. I recall that I shrunk back from his bedside as I looked at the site of his surgery. On another occasion he gave me his old .22 caliber, squirrel-hunting rifle. That was a prized possession of mine for several years. Eventually Grandpa lapsed into a coma and died a few days later. I recall when we received the dreaded early-morning phone call that he had passed. I also remember being so distraught over his death that although I accompanied my parents and Steve to the funeral home in Columbus, I could not bear to go in to the actual funeral.

My grandmother Clara "Kitty" Coons died in late July 1967 just barely after I had graduated from Wabash College. She was my beloved grandmother who spoiled me rotten. She had not remarried after Grandfather Merle had died and she was so proud of her two grandsons that she never missed an occasion to brag about us. While I was at Wabash she did my laundry and had me over every Sunday evening for dinner.

I recall that Kitty developed a slight tremor near the end of my spring semester. She lost weight and began to drop things but was adept at hiding her new disability. I think her next symptom was double vision caused by weakness of her extra-ocular muscles which made one eye deviate laterally. This prompted a trip to her doctor who immediately hospitalized her for a workup. Metastatic brain cancer was discovered but the primary tumor was never located. Over the next week or so she went downhill rapidly. One after another her cranial nerves failed to function and then she lapsed into a coma and died. I recall sitting at her bedside, holding her hand, and telling her I loved her. I think she squeezed by hand in response, but I was never certain. Her death was a grievous loss to me as I loved her deeply.

My Grandmother Richman died 13 months later just after I had completed my first year of medical school. She had developed a primary liver cancer which was thought to be a sequelae of serum hepatitis which she had contracted after a blood transfusion in 1947 when she was in Germany. Her funeral is a blur to me but I recall a terrifying ride back to Indianapolis from Columbus, Indiana. My first wife and I rode with my Uncle Bruce and Aunt Frances as they sped to the airport in order to catch a plane back to Oklahoma City. I think we sped along at 90 miles an hour and passed every car in our path. Uncle Bruce changed lanes abruptly in order not to hit a car in front of us. My first wife and I held hands for dear life in the back seat. It was a white-knuckle ride, but we arrived safely in time for Bruce and Frances to catch their plane flight.

Was I able to deal with death at this point? Not quite. I finally was able to grieve the death of Grandmother Coons while I was in psychotherapy during the fall of 1968.

I do recall a death of another med student's patient during my first clinical rotation during my junior year. Jeff's patient had had a massive stroke. During that first rotation we all learned how to keep electrolytes balanced while administering IV fluids. The supervising resident said that Jeff's patient died in "perfect electrolyte balance." Small comfort for that patient's family!

During my internship at Methodist Hospital we interns and residents shared the Kellys (the area of our on-call rooms, so called because the Kelly green color of our surgical scrubs) with chaplaincy students who were on call and came to every Code Blue. They were always present when patients died and were very helpful in dealing with families. I shared a number of calls with Stan, one of the chaplaincy students, and we had many late-night bull sessions, some of which included the topic of patient deaths.

In the spring of 1972 during my internship year I was on call around the time of the spring solstice in March. I remember this so clearly because the setting sun was coming from due west and shone into the room of my newly deceased patient, an elderly female. I was very comfortable in dealing with the death of this patient who had lived a long productive life. Her husband talked lovingly of his wife with his back to the window as the setting sun finally dipped below the horizon. I had finally done it. I was now comfortable with death. It was no longer to be feared.

SAVING LIVES

Medicine is all about saving lives, right? Actually the nuts and bolts of medicine is treating chronic illnesses and improving a person's quality of life.

As a psychiatrist, I'm sure that I have saved some lives, but how many, I have no idea. Psychiatrists save lives by preventing suicide and treating severe psychoses, but it's difficult to know just how many lives we have saved because it is often a team effort involving physicians, nurses, social workers, and other mental health professionals.

On two memorable occasions I'm certain that I saved a life. The first occasion occurred when I was an intern at Methodist Hospital in Indianapolis. On that particular day I was sauntering down a hospital hall, probably in route to a patient's room. Out of one patient's room raced a nurse looking for a doctor, any doctor, and I happened to be it. This patient had been hospitalized because of a severe electrical burn on his lower arm near his wrist and his radial artery had just eroded through and was spurting out bright red blood with each heartbeat. What was I to do? I wasn't a surgeon, had no surgical tools, much less any idea how to use them to stop an extremely serious arterial bleed. At this point my Boy Scout first aid training kicked in and I applied pressure to his brachial artery by pressing down tightly against his humerus bone in his upper arm. That maneuver quickly stopped the bleeding and I held on for dear life while the nurse raced to get his surgeon who arrived in minutes and proceeded to repair the artery.

In the second instance I was driving in southwestern Indiana and on my way to scuba dive in a local coal mining pit. I passed a vehicle which was in a ditch by the side of the road and noticed that steam or smoke was coming from the engine compartment. Sensing that this crash had just occurred moments before, I parked my car on the side of the road, and went to investigate. The vehicle was on its side, and sure enough, a man was trapped inside. He was barely conscious and was bleeding from his nose and mouth. I knew he had to be rescued immediately before a fire started which would have engulfed him in flames. I jerked upward on the driver's side door, but it would not budge. I looked around and by this time several onlookers had arrived. I asked someone to call 911 and pleaded with them to help me. Two men came over and with our joint effort we were able to rip the door open. We pulled the driver from the wreckage to a safe distance from his vehicle. I turned him on his side and proceeded to clear his mouth of blood so he would not aspirate. At that moment emergency medical personnel arrived and took over.

As a physician I had assumed that I would save a lot of lives in the emergency room but that was not the case. In these two memorable instances lives were saved well away from the emergency room doors. There was no time to think. I just acted automatically as I had been trained. I never suspected that my Boy Scout first aid training would help me as a physician.

LOSING LIVES

I was lucky on my junior and senior rotations in medical school that no one died under my care. This was not true during my internship, however.

Probably the hardest experience I ever had was seeing a young person die. This happened three times during my internship in 1971.

The first occurred during my emergency room rotation during the first month or two while I was at Methodist Hospital in Indianapolis. A young man was brought to the emergency department with acute left upper abdominal pain. He was to start college that fall and was only eight or nine years younger than I. His family physician had suspected a splenic rupture since his patient had been recovering from a case of acute mononucleosis. His patient was quite pale and in acute shock. The ER staff physician had multiple IVs started in order to administer fluids and whole blood. Despite our best efforts this young man went downhill, had a cardiorespiratory arrest, and died. We were at a loss to explain his death but a postmortem examination revealed not a ruptured spleen but a massive bilateral pulmonary embolism. This was before the days of pulmonary angiography, CT scans, and abdominal ultrasound. Had these tests been available at the time we might have saved his life with emergency surgery.

The second occurrence happened while I was covering night call for the Medicine Service. A young woman who had just delivered a baby had been admitted for disseminated intravascular coagulation (DIC), most likely of obstetric origin. The prognosis for DIC at that time was exceedingly grim as practically everyone died. Despite the best efforts of her physicians and consulting specialists she was expected to die that evening. It was exceedingly lonely for me as her treating physicians and consultants left for the night one by one. I was to watch their patient and pull the plug on her respirator as soon as her heart stopped beating. As the minutes and hours crept by, the nursing staff became restless and impatient and wanted me to pull the plug, but her heart kept beating strongly. When her heart finally stopped, I pulled the plug and pronounced her dead.

Later during my internship we lost a middle-aged woman on the Surgery Service from a massive upper gastrointestinal bleed. Not long afterwards we were able to save a patient with a massive lower intestinal bleed. I can't recall how many pints of blood we gave this person but in the end we were triumphant. Had fiber-optic colonoscopies been available at the time we would have been successful much sooner.

Death is no stranger to physicians, but when a patient dies, it is almost always a traumatic experience for the doctor because we have feelings and care about the survival for our patients.

CHAPTER 7

PSYCHIATRY

"As a second year psychiatric resident I saw my first person with multiple personality, now known as dissociative identity disorder."

CARTER HOSPITAL

From 1975 when I finished my psychiatry residency until 1995 I was a member of the Psychiatry Department at Indiana University School of Medicine in Indianapolis, Indiana. My faculty position was on the medical staff at Larue D. Carter Memorial Hospital, a state teaching and research psychiatric hospital on the campus of the Indiana University Medical Center, about one mile west of downtown Indianapolis. During the first 15 years that I was at Carter I was on the Inpatient Service, first on the Adult Female Service and then on the Adult Service after the male and female services merged.

When I joined the Female Service, I was one of four psychiatrists who had inpatient treatment teams. Dr. Patricia Sharpley was the head of the female service and Drs. Vincent Alig, Philip Morton, and I headed up the other three inpatient treatment teams. We each had a psychiatric resident, social worker, and medical student on our treatment teams, that is when there were enough residents to go around and there were fewer and fewer as the years wore on due to the increasing number of services and demands on residents both on and off campus. I had some great residents on my service, a few of whom went on to faculty positions both in our department and in other psychiatry departments around the country.

As a junior faculty member, I had a good opportunity at Carter Hospital to advance myself in the psychiatry department. My interest in the dissociative disorders enabled me to get in on the ground floor of some exciting research, but more about that later. I will say that my research and publishing in academic journals, teaching, and service enabled me to rise through the ranks from assistant professor to full professor over the course of 19 years. It was a slow slog, however, since my first paper in a refereed journal was not published until 1980. It was a review article on multiple personality which went through many revisions and was submitted to several journals before it was finally accepted as the lead article in the *Journal of Clinical Psychiatry*. I didn't know it at the time that most review articles were invited. Once I started publishing, I had the strong support and mentorship of Donald Moore, M.D., superintendent of Carter Hospital, and both Drs. Joyce and Iver Small, who headed the Research Service at Carter.

Carter Hospital had a strong Social Work Department. I had wonderful social workers on the Adult Service. From my residency days, they included Ruth, Dick, Carol, and Judi. They were responsible for interviewing family members about both the patient's psychiatric history and family history. We had an equally strong Psychology Department who would step in and administer psychological testing if requested. Victor, Art, Haya, and Finley were even co-authors on some of my published papers.

I transferred to the Carter Outpatient Service after 15 years on the Inpatient Service. While there, I continued my Dissociative Disorders Clinic which I had established about 10 years previously. The clinic offered expert consultation to dissociative disorder patients, their therapists, and treatment of some dissociative disorder patients. While on the Adult Service I had only staffed one resident at a time, but in the Outpatient Service I had several residents to staff since the university outpatient psychiatric services also included the Long Adult Psychiatry Clinic. During this period of time I worked closely with Susan and Rita, both social workers. My psychiatric colleague, Dr. Mary Ann Hoffman completed the complement to a very busy outpatient service at Carter Hospital.

I retired from Carter in 1995 because both my parents were quite ill from emphysema and I needed more time to help care for them. I remained with the Psychiatry Department, however, and continued to do forensic psychiatry which I had begun some years earlier while I was on the Adult Inpatient Service. This part-time work afforded me the time necessary to take care of my patients. Sadly the Carter Outpatient Clinic survived only a short time after Carter Hospital moved from West 10ᵗʰ Street to the former VA Hospital buildings on Cold Springs Road in Indianapolis. Change was in the air, with state budget cutbacks for mental health service. Carter Hospital would never again be the teaching and research bastion of the state hospital system as it was in the mid to late twentieth century.

MULTIPLE PERSONALITY

As a second year psychiatric resident I saw my first person with multiple personality, now known as dissociative identity disorder. She presented with phobic symptoms, but hinted she might have more than one personality. Although I had never before seen anyone with this unusual disorder, I recalled that two years earlier I had heard a case presentation about this condition at the Purdue Student Health Center. I didn't know how to diagnose her, but she had amnesia so I sent her for psychological testing. Her testing did not show any signs of physically based amnesia but the psychologists were just as puzzled as I was. Summarizing their report, they said I had a "good referral question" because they couldn't answer it even after 18 hours of testing. What was I to make of this? Finally three months after I had begun to see her, I saw an alternate personality and she sent shivers up my spine and made the hair of my arms stand on end. She had a different voice, different mannerisms, different ideas, even a different transference towards me.

Our encounters over the next two years stimulated a career's worth of investigation and study. I met Dr. Cornelia Wilbur, Sybil's therapist, at our residents' luncheon after she had presented Psychiatry Grand Rounds. Connie gave me advice that is just as valid today as it was then. I would learn what it was like to have multiple personality from my patient. She would be my teacher, if I was willing to listen. I did, and my patient taught me.

I gave my first Grand Rounds on multiple personality in 1975. I began to consult with other clinicians, such as Ralph Allison, M.D., from California. At that time, if you had seen one case of multiple personality, you were an expert, so in 1978 Ralph invited me to present at the American Psychiatric Association Annual Meeting. I continued presenting in the APA's Meeting workshops on multiple personality until 1986. When the newly formed International Society for the Study of Multiple Personality and Dissociation began workshops on multiple personality in 1984, I began teaching at those.

I published my first paper on multiple personality in 1980 and continued publishing on the subject for most of my career. I started a Dissociative Disorders Clinic at Carter Hospital and over the course of about 15 years saw about 400 individuals with various types of dissociative disorders including dissociative identity disorder, dissociative amnesia, dissociative fugue, depersonalization disorder, and dissociative disorder not otherwise specified. The vast majority of these patients were referred to me by other therapists for evaluation. To date I have published 140 journal articles, book chapters, books, letters to the editor, and book reviews, many of them on multiple personality or dissociative identity disorder.

As a second year resident in psychiatry, I could not have foreseen any of this. I am truly humbled, tankful, and gratified that I have had such an opportunity. Becoming an expert on the dissociative disorders enabled me to contribute to the formation of a field of psychiatry, help many suffering people, and rise through the academic ranks.

HOMOSEXUALITY

As a child I heard words like "queer," "fag," "fairy," and "homo." Boys called other boys these words and I had no idea what they meant, although I knew it wasn't good; it was an insult. In junior high a male classmate exhibited behaviors associated with being gay, but I still didn't get it.

I finally figured out in high school what it meant to be gay or lesbian. In fact, I lived next door to a lesbian couple, both public librarians, and they seemed normal enough. However, my only knowledge of male homosexuality was reading about the promiscuous behavior of gay males in California bathhouses.

As a freshman college student, a fellow pledge brother discussed his drug abuse and homosexuality with me as we were guarding the campus against DePauw intruders the week before the Wabash/DePauw football game. He didn't return to college for his second semester. Was it because of his drug abuse or did he feel anxious about being in an all-male college which celebrated masculinity but devalued the gay lifestyle? I'll never know for certain.

During my second year in medical school we were given a class in sexuality which included material on homosexuality. This was in the late 1960s when homosexuality was considered a mental disorder. Early in my psychiatry residency homosexuality continued to be diagnosed as a mental disorder and treatment was advocated for the condition.

As a third year psychiatry resident, I finally got it. I was treating a homosexual male patient who loved his partner. They were in a long-term relationship, just like straight marital couples. What an epiphany! About the same time the American Psychiatric Association dropped homosexuality as a diagnosis. As I continued in my career I found out that a number of psychiatry residents and colleagues were gay, and they were normal.

In my early 40s my second wife and I joined a liberal Methodist church that had a few gay couples, and they were normal too. Their attempt to become a reconciling congregation (accepting of LGBT persons) went down in ignominious defeat in the mid-1990s, however.

Fast forward to my mid 40s when I learned that three extended family members were gay. Another mind-shattering epiphany!

Are we making any progress? Well, some. Our church recently became a reconciling congregation. A family member and his partner are having their relationship blessed by an Episcopal priest.

DEPRESSION

I became depressed during medical school, not once but twice. Medical school was quite different from college in more ways than one. During the first year and a half there was a vast amount of material to memorize and regurgitate for tests. In addition at Indiana University Medical School in Indianapolis, then the nation's largest medical school, there was little time to interact with the professors as I had at Wabash College. These medical school professors had too many students to have any time for individual attention. In addition they were busy with their individual research projects.

My first depression occurred during the summer after my first year. It was preceded by a viral pharyngitis and occurred while I was working as an orderly for the Surgery Department. I had been told that I would get to observe surgery, but instead I was relegated to transporting patients to and from surgery. What a letdown! My depression, unlike the majority of depressions, had hypersomnia as a major symptom. I slept every chance I got. When I began coursework for the fall semester, I could not concentrate. I'd look at a page in a textbook and just could not focus. I was incredibly fatigued. Everything was an effort. It felt like a mountain that I could not scale. When I almost had an automobile accident on my way to school and thought, "I don't care if I live or die," I knew I had to see a psychiatrist. Fortunately there were psychiatrists at school who were willing to see medical students and I was sent to see Dr. Ed Tyler, a child psychiatrist at Riley Hospital. Over the course of the next several months I ventilated my frustrations about medical school (A pharmacology professor refused to see me to talk about test results.), my first marriage (My wife was finding it difficult to cope with a medical student who spent the majority of his time studying.), and the loss of my grandmother a year previously. I tried the antidepressant Tofranil, but had to stop it because of an episode of paroxysmal atrial tachycardia, so bad that I couldn't stand up without nearly fainting. My depression suddenly disappeared when Ed suggested electroconvulsive therapy. After that I recall walking across campus and kicking a tin can as hard as I could because I was so angry. My angry depression had been externalized and I began to feel much better. I was able to resume studying and enjoyed the rest of the year, especially the second semester when we began to study clinical medicine.

I began my third year on a clinical neurology rotation which I thoroughly enjoyed. I dropped out of my psychiatry rotation, however, on the first day because my assigned faculty was an administrator who was nowhere to be found. His patient notes were incomprehensible because of his atrocious handwriting. What was I to do, since I was interested in psychiatry as a career? Two years earlier I had been unimpressed with our freshman psychiatry lectures because our text, *An Introduction to the Science of Human Behavior,* by the Psychiatry Department chairman, John Nurnberger, Sr., and two of his colleagues had little do with clinical psychiatry. It was all about neuroscience and was far more suited to a beginning neuroscience Ph.D. candidate rather than a beginning medical student. I dropped out of school for a day or two, but rationality was restored when I finally realized that dropping out meant I'd probably have to go to Vietnam and kill people. I wanted to help people, not shoot them. I got back into therapy immediately, resumed my studies, and enjoyed the rest of my junior year.

The statistics on having a third depression after having had two episodes are grim, but I thankfully have never had a third depression. Over the years I've looked for a history of depression in my family and found a little. My mother had a late-life depression precipitated by steroid administration after she almost died from emphysema. There was a postpartum depression in an extended family member, but nothing else. In retrospect I think my depression was mostly caused by external factors such as the losses that I have described. Having suffered from depression has given me more empathy for my depressed patients.

FORENSIC PSYCHIATRY

As mentioned previously, I began working in 1995 part-time by doing forensic psychiatry. Initially I worked with another psychiatrist and two psychologists in the Forensic Psychiatry Clinic in the Psychiatry Department at Indiana University School of Medicine. In 2005 I left that clinic and continued part-time forensic work in private practice.

My interest in forensic psychiatry goes back to my days in residency when I consulted at the Reception Diagnostic Center in Plainfield under the tutelage of William Fisher, M.D. Early in my career at Carter Hospital I had a few more cases, most notably a woman who killed her physically abusive husband.

As my expertise in the dissociative disorders field became more-widely known, my practice of forensic psychiatry exploded, first in the civil area of malpractice and then in the criminal arena. Eventually I started receiving non-dissociative cases in both civil and criminal areas. By the time of my retirement I had testified as an expert witness in 28 Indiana counties and 15 different states. Most of my cases in the civil area involved medical malpractice and most of my cases in the criminal area involved murder or attempted murder, which, of course, were the most serious offenses. In the criminal area I usually testified about competency to stand trial, sanity at the time of the crime, and mitigating circumstances.

My work in forensic psychiatry was vastly different from my work in general clinical psychiatry where I did both psychotherapy and medication management. In forensic psychiatry the client is the court or an attorney, either the prosecutor or the defense attorney. In these situations there is no doctor-patient confidentiality and no treatment is provided.

What I found during the years that I practiced forensic psychiatry was the judges and attorneys were quite adept at picking out mentally ill offenders. What they wanted to know was whether their client's mental illness rendered them incompetent to stand trial or whether the defendant was not culpable for his or her crime because of mental illness. In some cases, although the defendant was found guilty, their mental illness presented an important mitigating factor to be considered in their sentencing.

In my years of experience with mentally ill offenders I developed a profound empathy for them. They were like any other mentally ill person, except that they just happened to be in trouble with the law. In my work with them I discovered that they were treated much differently from the mentally ill not within the criminal justice system. They were often denied the most basic of both medical and psychiatric services. For example, I came across one inmate in a county jail who was not on medication for his HIV infection. In another county jail an inmate languished for months in a severely psychotic state before he was transferred to an appropriate state forensic psychiatric facility for treatment. In the Indiana Department of Correction I came across severely mentally ill offenders who were mislabeled as malingers and denied care. Others were denied appropriate medication because of the DOC's overly restrictive pharmacological formularies. Still others were incarcerated in what would be considered inhuman conditions.

Although it's sometimes difficult to know whether or when I have saved a life as a clinical psychiatrist, I'm confident that I have participated in saving the lives of severely mentally ill offenders. In one case, based upon my testimony and other circumstances, our Indiana governor commuted a death sentence of a multiple murderer to life imprisonment. In still other cases death sentences were not pursued because of the offenders' severe mental illness. It is gratifying to help the most severely mentally ill defendants receive more appropriate sentences.

CHAPTER 8

HOBBIES

"My two favorite hobbies are photography and travel which I frequently combine on short trips, vacations, or junkets, as Liz sometimes calls them."

TRAVEL AND VACATIONS

A favorite hobby of mine is travel. I have traveled to all 50 states and 45 countries.

My zest for travel grew out of a few family vacations when I was a child. One of my first memories is of not being allowed to go in the water at Indiana Dunes State Park when I was a toddler. During the next few years until I was about 5 or 6 we vacationed at Big Star Lake in Michigan. We rented a cottage while my father was performing his Army Reserve duty at Camp Grayling, Michigan. For several years after that we vacationed during the summers at the Stony Ridge Hotel on Lake Tippecanoe in Kosciusko County, Indiana.

When I was age 12 our family visited Washington, D.C., Mount Vernon, Monticello, and Williamsburg, Virginia. On our way out we drove along the Blue Ridge Parkway. That particular vacation intensely fueled my interest in travel.

It wasn't until after my junior year in high school that I finally got to go west of the Mississippi when I received a National Science Foundation scholarship to the Indiana University Geologic Field Station in the Tobacco Root Mountains in southwestern Montana. That particular trip piqued my interest in mountains and the Western United States to which I've returned many times.

Prior to my marriage to Liz, I took two Wabash College Alumni trips with my parents, one to Switzerland and the other to Tahiti, Australia, and New Zealand. The Swiss Alps and the Southern Alps in New Zealand were mesmerizing. In 1980 my father and I made a grand tour of Europe to visit several WWII sites where he had been stationed. We landed in Frankfort, Germany, rented a car, then we drove through the Ardennes Forest, Germany, Lichtenstein, Switzerland, Italy, Monaco, France, and then back to Germany. What a thrill it was to see the Eifel Tower, Notre Dame, Chartres Cathedral, the Roman Coliseum, Trevi Fountain, Venice, the Leaning Tower of Pisa, and the Swiss

Alps including Gotthard Pass. The WWII sites we visited included Montmarte in Paris, Arles, and Normandy. We even found the exact farmhouse where Dad was stationed near Versailles in southern France.

Since marrying Liz we have traveled all over Western Europe, the Caribbean, and South America. Some of our favorite places in South America include Machu Picchu in Peru, Rio de Janeiro, Buenos Aires, Lake Titicaca, and the Lakes Region and Andes between Argentina and Chile. We have visited numerous Islands in the Caribbean while sailing on Windjammer Cruises.

I have many places to visit on my bucket list and these include Mexico City, Venezuela, Columbia, Kenya, South Africa, Japan, and China. Bon Voyage and *Gute Fhart*!

PHOTOGRAPHY

My two favorite hobbies are photography and travel which I frequently combine on short trips, vacations, or junkets, as Liz sometimes calls them.

My first camera was a fixed-focus Kodak Brownie Target-Six-20 box camera. I wish I still had it as it would be an antique now. My second camera was also a Kodak with a bellows focus and it was given to me by my grandfather Richman. Both of these cameras used Kodak 620 roll film. My third camera was a Kodak Pony 135 which used slide film. I used that camera from about age 12 until I got married at age 22. I'm probably most proud of the black and white print that I took at Williamsburg, Virginia just as a cannon was going off. The picture captured the smoke coming from the barrel of the cannon and convinced me that I wanted to pursue photography.

My mother and me in Williamsburg, Virginia

After I married at age 22 I purchased a Mamiya-Sekor through-the-lens (SLR) camera and this camera lasted many years until it broke and I bought a Canon SLR camera. It took me a long time to switch to digital photography because the cameras were expensive and of low quality at first, but I finally succumbed in 2005 and bought a digital.

For most of my life I have avidly taken scenic photographs. It's only recently that I have graduated to taking photographs of people and I find that I have a knack for it. I also found that the best way to photograph people is to sit quietly and use a telephoto lens to capture people unawares as they go about their activities. I might have been a good spy!

I love to be out at sunrise and sunset to photograph the vivid hues of crimson, fuchsia, pink, and blue in the clouds and sky surrounding the rising and setting sun. I loved being at the shoreline of Caribbean islands to capture the azure and teal colors of the ocean. I like to capture the reflections of autumn-colored Midwestern trees in lakes and ponds. It's like an impressionist painting. When taking close-up photos I like to focus in and capture the simplicity of nature's abstractions. When I am out among Nature's creations, I am enthralled by the splendor and beauty of our planet.

I love to travel on narrow highways such as in the Grand Staircase Escalante National Monument in Utah and photograph the sinuous path of US Route 89. Its grandiosity rivals that of the Grand Canyon which I have photographed on days of splendid sunshine and days of mist and frequent raindrops.

I love to walk on trails in the woods, out in the desert, or along the seashore. At such times I thrill to hear the melodious chirps and trills of songbirds and watch birds of prey soar in the sky above me. I also like to photograph small furry animals such as chipmunks and ground squirrels. Once when I was in Glacier National park, I was able to photograph mountain goats. They were so close that I could have reached out and touched them. For obvious reasons my photos of bears and wolves have been taken from a long distance through a telephoto lens.

Although I've entered photographs in a number of contests, I've never won more than third prize. It is very gratifying, however, to hear numerous compliments about my photos when I post them on Facebook or exhibit them at church.

GENEALOGY

Beside photography and travel, genealogy is one of my most favorite hobbies. I started doing genealogy in my mid-twenties after I had finished medical school. I'd already had considerable exposure to genealogy in my family. When my brother was in high school, he started asking questions about great grandparents and other relatives for a project in school. His questions stimulated a lot of interest in our family by both sets of grandparents. Kitty, my grandmother Coons, started corresponding with her brother, my great Uncle Ed, in Oklahoma and my Richman grandparents began correspondence with distant relatives, took trips to the east coast to do research, and even hired a genealogist. My dad picked up the genealogy bug and started doing research on the Coons and the paternal side Van Cleave families in Tennessee and North Carolina.

When I developed an interest in genealogy a great deal of research on our family had already been accomplished. What I set out to do was verify what my family had done and to collect anything and everything I could find on all of my direct ancestors. In the process I was able to extend our family tree back along numerous branches. In that process I discovered that many of my ancestors had written diaries, letters, and other information about what their lives were like and what they had done. In the end I was able to publish two books with this material. One of the books, *Letters Home from a WWII Black Panther Artilleryman* (Bloomington, Indiana: iUniverse, 2012), contains my entire father's letters to my mother during WWII. The other book, *In Their Own Words: Hoosier Ancestor and Family Journeys* (Bloomington, Indiana: iUniverse, 2010), contains writings by many of my direct ancestors with Hoosier connections.

Collecting all of this genealogical information has involved countless hours doing internet research on my computer and library research at the Indiana State Library. Moreover, I have made many road trips to other states such as Iowa, Kentucky, Tennessee, North Carolina, New Jersey, and Pennsylvania, just to name a few. My wife Liz has been very gracious and has put up with my peripatetic wanderings, although she considered some of my trips only "semi-authorized" because she is loath to lose her cook and bedmate for a week at a time. She has also been gracious in listening at the dinner table to the details of my genealogical research.

I have tried to involve Liz in genealogy by working on her family tree and we have gone on several trips together to northern Indiana, Ohio, and Illinois to research various branches of her family. I have been pretty successful in this endeavor, but I can tell when she is tiring of the hunt and looks bored or nearly goes to sleep in library family history rooms. She has been able to stay in decent hotels and eat out in nice restaurants and even has gone on some shopping forays, so all is not lost as far as she is concerned. One thing that both she and I have enjoyed is viewing our ancestral land holdings and finding their graves through our "cemetery crawling" adventures.

So far I have accumulated one full four-drawer file cabinet full of genealogical material. Although this may sound like a lot of information to a non-genealogist, I have one genealogist friend, Francine, who has three full file cabinets. Another friend, Karen, has 300,000 individuals in her Ancestry computer database, compared to my measly 30,000!

All in all, genealogy has been a very interesting and worthwhile hobby. Now I just have to identify a younger cousin who wants to inherit all of my research information. I think my father would be proud of my research extending our family tree.

READIN'

My mother read children's books to me as a preschooler. I have a vague memory of being nestled in bed under the covers at bedtime with her reading to me while I looked at the pictures in the oversized children's book that she was holding.

In the first and second grade I graduated to the *Dick and Jane* readers. Dick and Jane were brother and sister. They had a little sister Sally, Spot the dog, and Puff the cat. I became such a good reader that I could devour an entire Dick and Jane book in about 30 minutes.

"See Spot run. Run, Spot, Run!" Remember? An entire generation of Baby Boomers learned to read this sanitized book series.

I also recall that my teachers in the first and second grade read Charles Major's *Bears of Blue River* (New York: MacMillan, 1901) and *Uncle Tom Andy Bill: A Story of Bears and Indian Treasure* (New York: MacMillan, 1908) to us during story hour. To a Hoosier boy interested in early nineteenth century Indiana pioneers these stories about life in the Indiana woodlands along Blue River were enthralling.

Later on in grade school I latched on to my brother's biographies of famous Americans published by Bobbs-Merrill. This was a series of books about Davy Crockett, Buffalo Bill, Kit Carson, Daniel Boone, George Washington, Abraham Lincoln, Thomas Edison, etc. The Childhood of Famous Americans series also carried books about famous American women such as Clara Barton, Dolly Madison, and Betsy Ross.

When I reached high school I was fascinated by the novels of Ernest Hemingway and John Steinbeck. My first Steinbeck book was *The Grapes of Wrath* (New York: Viking Press, 1939). I was totally blown away by the ending. Who can forget Rose of Sharon Joad Rivers breast-feeding a starving stranger?

> "Rose of Sharon loosened one side of the blanket and
> bared her breast. 'You got to,' she said. She squirmed

136

closer and pulled his head close. 'There!' she said. 'There.'"

I loved Steinbeck's *Cannery Row* (New York: Viking Press, 1945) and I couldn't put down *Travels with Charley: In Search of America* (New York: Viking Press, 1962) a nonfiction piece about Steinbeck exploring the United States in his camper with his dog Charley. Poor Charley, who knew what to do when confronted with a fire hydrant or a sapling, hadn't the vaguest idea of what to do when confronted with a giant Sequoia. I think this was a great disappointment to Steinbeck as well as his readers, including me. Or maybe Charley wasn't the smartest dog on the block:

> "Once Charley fell in love with a dachshund, a romance racially unsuitable, physically ridiculous, and mechanically impossible. But all these problems Charley ignored. He loved deeply and tried dogfully."

Ernest Hemingway's novels were equally enthralling. *A Farewell to Arms* (New York: Scribner, 1928) and *For Whom the Bell Tolls* (New York: Scribner Press, 1940) were heartbreaking books about World War I and the Spanish Civil War. I was captivated by *The Old Man and the Sea* (New York: Scribner, 1952) and was devastated when Hemingway put a shotgun to his mouth and blew his brains out at his home in Ketchum, Idaho in the summer of 1961.

Other great novels I read as an adolescent were Harper Lee's *To Kill a Mockingbird* (New York: Lippincott, 1960) and the all-time classic about adolescent males, *The Catcher in the Rye* (New York: Little, Brown, 1951) by J.D. Salinger. I can't get Holden Caufield's friends, pimply-faced Ackley and the ever urbane Stradlater, out of my mind, especially Stradlater's grody razor. That's why I don't loan out my razor, not even to my beloved wife. Her admission to me years later that she had used my razor several times still doesn't sit well with me!

Another topic that has interested me all of my life has been stories of adventure. I devoured books such as Thor Heyerdahl's *Kon Tiki*, (Australia: George Allen, 1950) Alfred Lansing's *Endurance: Shackleton's Incredible Voyage* (New York: McGraw Hill, 1959), and Saint-Exupery's *Wind, Sand and Stars* (Reynal and Hitchcock, 1939).

Books about animals, especially dogs, fascinate me. I loved *Marley and Me* (New York: Harper Collins, 2005) by John Grogan. I read every one of James Herriot's books about being a veterinarian in rural England. If I hadn't become a physician, I surely would have been a veterinarian.

I discovered a gold mine when I found Mark Twain. My grandmother Richman gave me a complete set of Twain when I was in junior high. My favorites at that time, of course, were *The Adventures of Tom Sawyer* (American Publishing Company, 1876) and *The Adventures of Huckleberry Finn* (American Publishing Company, 1885). As an adult I couldn't put down his non-fiction works *Life on the Mississippi* (Boston: James Osgood, 1883) and *The Innocents Abroad* (American Publishing Company, 1869).The latter book is a deliciously satirical sailing adventure via steamship around the Mediterranean Sea and Holy Land.

Probably my greatest love is reading biographies and memoirs. That's where I started out in childhood and my curiosity about human nature has only fueled this passion. I've read more about Franklin Roosevelt than you can shake a stick at. I think books about Roosevelt are particularly interesting because they involve a figure larger than life during the dark days of World War II.

I got interested in memoirs while participating in a memoir group. I couldn't put down Mary Karr's *The Liars' Club*. Her use of prose and psychological mindedness is astounding:

> "A dysfunctional family is any family with more than
> one person in it."

Tobias Wolff's *This Boy's Life* (New York: Grove Press, 1989), unlike *Catcher in the Rye*, is a true story about adolescence. I was saddened and angered when I read about Wolff's physical and mental abuse by his stepfather. I positively shivered when Wolff looked out the window of his apartment and aimed his loaded rifle at a man walking on the sidewalk a block away.

Jeannette Walls' *The Glass Castle* (New York: Scribner, 2005) recounts the author's childhood of poverty in Appalachia with little help from two very dysfunctional parents. Despite growing up in abject poverty with two screwed up parents, Wall's love unconditional love of humanity is striking:

> "You should never hate anyone, even your worst enemies. Everyone has something good about them. You have to find the redeeming quality and love the person for that."

In *Easter Everywhere* (Bloomsberry, 2008) by Darcy Steinke the author, a preacher's kid, grows up in the forests of Idaho. She rebels as an adolescent and loses her faith, only to regain it later in life:

> "Since I was a teenager I've lived in a world mostly devoid of divinity. But now I see the sacred includes not just churches but hospitals, highways, costume jewelry, garbage dumps, libraries, the cruising area of public parks. Also pet stores, subway platforms, Ferris wheels and rain storms."

In my study, I've got a stack of books to read, actually, two stacks. I'd better stop writing and get another book started.

WRITIN'

In 1967 with my newly minted bachelor's degree I rejoiced that I would never have to write another paper. This naive young man was going into medicine. During my high school years I wrote countless themes and as a college student I had penned numerous papers. Part of my loathing of writing papers was my lack of typing skills. I am a "hunt and peck" typist who uses one or two fingers.

What I didn't know or expect was my entry into academic medicine upon the completion of my psychiatry residency. In academic medicine those who want to get promoted in academic rank must write papers. It's "publish or perish."

It took me five years to publish my first paper, a review article on multiple personality disorder, one of my research interests. To write this paper I took a course on writing professionally. It was offered by a research librarian at Wishard Memorial Hospital in Indianapolis. No one told me was that review papers were almost always written by invited authors. Nevertheless my paper was accepted by the *Journal of Clinical Psychiatry* and, incredibly, it was a lead article in its issue, a real compliment.

Since my first paper was published in 1980 I have published over 125 journal articles, book chapters, books, letters to the editor, and book reviews. The task of publishing was made much easier when my wife and I bought our first computer and printer, an IBM dual floppy disk drive in the mid-1980s. These two machines set us back $5000.

Although I am proud that my publishing in psychiatry enabled me to obtain the rank of full professor in 1994, I am most proud of the three books that I wrote during semi-retirement. My first book, *In Their Own Words: Hoosier Ancestor and Family Journeys* (Bloomington, Indiana: iUniverse) was published in 2009. It consists of letters, diaries, journal entries, etc. of many of my direct ancestors who had Hoosier connections. Among the more interesting chapters are the Civil War letters of my great great-grandfather and a description of the Flick Trial, one of the Nuremburg War Crimes Trials, written by my grandfather Frank Richman, an Indiana Supreme Court Justice who presided at that trial. The book also contains the diary kept by Grandfather Richman when he sailed down the Ohio and Mississippi Rivers with diesel inventor Clessie Cummins in a sailboat hand-built by Mr. Cummins.

My second book, *Psychiatry in Indiana, the First 175 Years* (Bloomington, Indiana: iUniverse, 2010) was written with my coauthor wife. In our book we covered the history of psychiatry in Indiana beginning when Indiana was a territory in 1800 through 1975 when I became a faculty member in the Department of Psychiatry at Indiana University School of Medicine. We addressed Indiana's state mental hospitals, developmental disabilities facilities, private psychiatric facilities, community mental health centers, important Indiana psychiatrists and other mental health professionals, the Indiana Psychiatric Society, infamous historical Indiana patients, and a host of other topics. This book is truly unique.

My third book, *Letters Home from a WWII Black Panther Artilleryman* (Bloomington, Indiana: iUniverse, 2012) is an edited compilation of my father's WWII letters to my mother. It follows my father through his basic training, combat experience in Brittany, and post-WWII experiences near Marseilles and in Paris with the Criminal Investigation Division. I learned a great deal about my father from editing his letters.

My family loved *In Their Own Words* and *Letters Home*. My psychiatric colleagues were ecstatic about *Psychiatry in Indiana*.

As a graduating college student, never in the world would I have imagined that I would publish three books and have at least one more, a memoir, in the pipeline, but life usually brings some surprises. I leave you with one last remark: I'm still a "hunt and peck" typist.

THE GRUMPY GOURMET

I'm a decent cook, but that hasn't always been so. When I got married in 1981 I could cook a nice breakfast of bacon and eggs, toast, coffee, and orange juice. I could also grill steaks, chicken, and pork chops. For the pork chops and chicken I always used Uncle Bruce's Barbeque Sauce, an old family recipe purloined by my uncle from *Good Housekeeping*, I think. This limited repertoire helped me to snag a starving intern who became my wife. I learned to make these dishes by watching my mother cook and my father grill.

After we married, Liz and I shared cooking responsibilities. We would each cook dinner three days a week and one of us cleaned up the dishes after the other cooked. Almost immediately I felt I needed to enlarge my cooking repertoire, so I raided my mother's recipe file and began to cook recipes mainly from the *Better Homes and Gardens Cookbook*. I discovered that I liked cooking because I liked to eat. Cooking a recipe is really no different from performing a chemistry experiment. You just have to follow directions.

However, putting together more than one recipe and having all of them come out hot at the same time proved challenging, so challenging in fact that my wife Liz and my brother Steve nicknamed me "the Grumpy Gourmet" because I would get rather irritated if interrupted in the middle of fixing dinner. I couldn't converse amicably and cook at the same time. I needed to concentrate so I often curtly ordered everyone from the kitchen. Liz described this as "snarking and snapping."

Not all of my recipes ended on a successful note. Liz and I began to name the recipes we liked "keepers." I'm not certain what she called the ones she didn't like since she was usually diplomatic enough to keep that to herself.

As a budding cook I had to learn kitchen techniques of measuring, pouring, battering, frying, baking, etc. Probably the most hilarious was me trying to flour a cake pan. Having never observed anyone do this

I carefully greased the pan and then flicked flour here and there over the cake pan. Liz observed this and almost fell on the floor laughing. Having won several 4H awards for her baking as a teenager, she quickly taught me the correct technique. It was so easy to swirl flour around the cake pan, but this had never occurred to me.

I now consider myself to be an accomplished cook and I would describe my cooking as "down home." I try to avoid fats and cholesterol and strive to produce a balanced meal of meat, vegetables, and salad. I love deserts and can make some great ones, but we usually avoid these to minimize weight gain.

I'm organized but I don't keep recipes in a recipe box like my wife, mother, and grandmothers. I have eight three-ringed cookbooks in which recipes are neatly printed on 5x7 recipe cards. I have one each for appetizers and drinks, breads and rolls, salads, meats, fish and poultry, deserts, and two for vegetables, listed in alphabetical order, of course.

Did I mention that I'm seriously O-C [obsessive-compulsive]? I'm also an amicable cook most of the time now. Liz thinks I've gone from a "grumpy gourmet" to a "slightly crabby cook."

CHAPTER 9

OTHER FUN STUFF

"As a young faculty member I acquired the nickname
'Bone Doctor' from the nursing staff who had nicknamed
my hyperactive anorexic patient 'The Bionic Bone.'"

WINTERTIME FUN

Thank God for our family's photo archives. One photo taken in late fall 1946 when I was 18 months shows me toddling headlong and about to cross Riverview Drive in Indianapolis. This fearlessness towards automobiles ultimately persuaded my mother to buy me a harness and leash! Another picture taken when I was about four and a half shows my older brother and me standing in the snow in front of our house on Riverview Drive. Still another photo shows my dad perched on a sled and riding behind our TR-2 [Triumph] sports-car when we lived on Sherwood Drive near Williams Creek.

Although photos bring back memories, my fondest remembrances of winter are not documented with photographs.

When we lived on Sherwood Drive and had experienced an ample snow, all the neighborhood kids would congregate on a small hill next to the Dulin house and sled down towards Williams Creek. Some of us borrowed our dads' car wax and waxed our sleds' runners so we could speed down the hill even faster. Fortunately none of us landed in Williams Creek.

Another memory involves our family going to Grandmother Coons' farm home about seven miles south of Crawfordsville on State Road 47. While there one winter weekend when I was about seven we had a heavy snowstorm which snowed us in for three days until a plow could make it down from Crawfordsville. My brother and I were not heartbroken over our forced vacation from school, however. We each made a snow-fort and lobbed snowballs back and forth at each other.

Our family was very lucky that we could afford winter vacations in Florida. We have many pictures documenting our stays on Bradenton Beach and Sanibel Island from the time I was six months old until I was about twelve. I can still recall taking the ferry to Sanibel Island long before the bridge was built linking the island with the mainland on the Gulf coast.

When I was in the ninth grade our family moved to San Juan, Puerto Rico for a year. It was a tough year living in the tropics when the temperature hovered at about 85 year round, but someone had to do it.

My years at Wabash College in the late 60s brought more wintertime fun. I recall several all-campus snowball fights. Another particularly sharp memory was my having to ride the fraternity bicycle to the post office in downtown Crawfordsville in order to retrieve the fraternity mail, a two-mile round trip. This I did once in a frigid and blinding snowstorm. On my way back, someone reached out of his car window and stole my green freshman beanie or pot. I expect the thief got quite a surprise when he got home and smelled the pot which had been soaked with asafetida, a foul smelling chemical that used to be placed in a bag around someone's neck and used to ward off flu symptoms. One of the diabolical sophomores who supervised our pledge-ship had come up with the obnoxious idea of boiling our pots in a brew of asafetida and making us wear them for the rest of the semester. I did not mourn the loss of my pot!

Another great memory during my college years was sliding down the steep hill at Happy Hollow Park in West Lafayette, Indiana. I remember with great relish the looks on a small boy's face as I prepared to slide down on a snow saucer. "You're really going to get hurt, mister," he admonished. I understand that in recent years Purdue University students slide down this hill in purloined cafeteria trays.

A not-too-pleasant memory of winter fun was during the blizzard of '78 when my first wife and I were marooned for three days in our apartment in International Village in Speedway. We became so restless being housebound that my neighbor and I sledded down a hill in his small sailboat.

My final memory involves a 2002 snow-mobile adventure to West Yellowstone, Montana that my wife Liz and I took with the Ambassadair Travel Club. We stayed in a motel just outside Yellowstone National Park. Our first day of snowmobiling was fabulous as we traveled to a mountaintop where we could view the Grand Tetons from a distance. We were so warmly dressed that we could barely feel the sub-zero chill.

Trying to relieve oneself in that weather is another story which doesn't bear repeating since my wife was the main character in that episode. At the conclusion of the day we returned to a flat plain where we were allowed to race our snowmobiles as fast as they could go. I reached 60 MPH by my speedometer. Unfortunately I contracted a stomach virus and could not go out the next day when our group went into Yellowstone Park.

Hopefully the future will yield more wintertime fun.

THE RIVI

When I was about six our family joined the Riviera Club on the north side of Indianapolis. The Rivi had a giant outdoor swimming pool, so it was a great way to beat the oppressive summer heat and humidity, especially since our home lacked the modern convenience of air conditioning. All four of us family members tanned easily, so we didn't usually have to worry about sunburn if we took it easy and limited sun exposure during the early days of summer.

The pool had a high dive and a giant aluminum water slide kept cool by cold water cascading down its full length. It took me a couple of years to summon up enough courage to climb the steps of either and take the frightening plunge off the diving board or the rapid descent on the water slide. Many of my school chums also went to the Rivi where I took my first swimming lessons. I can still taste and smell the acrid chlorine! Later I took dancing lessons at the Rivi in Mrs. Gates' dancing class, but that is another terrifying story.

It took me many years to realize that what the Rivi lacked were kids and families of color. This deficiency was pointed out years later by Charles, a black member of a Bible study group that I joined in my late 30s. Charles and his Caucasian wife did not join the Rivi until a lawsuit alleging racial discrimination was settled out-of-court in 1982.

Although my parents were not prejudiced against black people, we lived on Indianapolis' north side in Washington Township and had little exposure to blacks during the 1950s. There was only one black child, the son of a physician, in my grade school. We had a black maid and we traveled through Indianapolis' near north side on the way to church, but those two experiences could hardly count as exposure.

I recall my mother telling me that there were separate restrooms and drinking fountains for blacks in the southern states through which we traveled on our way to Florida on winter vacations. This puzzled me. What I didn't know was that Blacks in these states could not sit at restaurant lunch counters and had to sit at the back of a bus. I recall being shocked when my deeply tanned father came back from Puerto Rico and was denied entrance into a Miami bar until he pealed back his watch wrist band and showed that he was white.

More shocks were to follow in high school. Although we were fully integrated at New Albany Senior High School, black and white students kept to themselves and the black students congregated around the school's trophy case. They were proud of their athletic achievements and at this time sports was about their only entre into white middle-class society. Just across the Ohio River in Louisville, segregation was still in full force. A bright spot was that my black high school peers in Louisville were the ones who took charge of demonstrations against segregation and sat in at lunch counters.

My education about the evils of segregation was continued at Wabash College where some of my classmates traveled to the South to participate in demonstrations against segregation. This is something that I did not do because I had to avoid arrests if I wanted to be admitted to medical school. We did have a few black students at Wabash, but not a single black student was in my 1971 graduating medical school class.

As an adult I have lived in two integrated neighborhoods. The first was the Butler-Tarkington Neighborhood and now we live in Pike Township. In Indianapolis we attend a racially integrated church which includes people of Asian, African, Latin, and European ancestry. This diversity creates a much richer worship environment.

It is now 2013, and, although we have come a long way, our American race relations have a long way to go to insure that future Trayvon Martins have a right to walk home unmolested as they carry their Skittles and iced tea.

SPORTS FANATIC

In grade school I remember being chosen last or next-to-last in every competitive game we played in gym. I could dodge those dodge balls as they hurtled toward me, but I was probably good at that because I was skinny as a rail and a tough target to hit. "String-bean" was my nickname at the time.

I can't ever recall catching a fly ball as an outfielder in a softball game or making a basket in a basketball game in gym class when I was in junior high and high school. I'm not bragging about this record. It is what it is. I do recall that I was able to climb a rope all the way to the top of the gym and do numerous chin-ups. That was probably not a great achievement because I had so little weight to lift against gravity.

Although I was told by my swimming instructor at the Riviera Club in Indianapolis that I might make a good competitive swimmer, because of my shyness, I did not try out for their swim team. No, I waited until the tenth grade in high school to try out. I attended the first practice of the season and everybody was swimming a mile, so I jumped in and proceeded to swim, first doing the crawl, then the breast stroke, then the side stroke, then the back stroke, and then the dog paddle. Finally the coach, who was absent the whole time, stuck his face in the pool area and mercifully ended the practice. I dressed and hobbled to my bus stop on rubbery legs. My legs were so weak that I could hardly board the bus. That experience ended my competitive swimming career!

At Wabash College we were required to take one year of physical education. In order to avoid further mortal embarrassment, I opted to join an individual program consisting of running laps, lifting weights and doing calisthenics. By this time my nickname was "the bod," spelled with a little 'b,' compared to my fraternity brother, Jan, a strapping six-foot-three football player who weighed twice as much as I. He was known as "the Bod," spelled with a capital "B."

Participation in sports certainly is not in my genes, since neither my mother nor my father played any kind of sports. In 1914 my grandfather, Merle Coons, was principal of the Wingate, Indiana High School, the year they won the state high school basketball championship. I have a photograph of him with the winning basketball team, but to my best knowledge that is the closest he ever came to a basketball.

Merle Coons with the Wingate Indiana High School basketball team

I recently found out that my other grandfather, Frank Richman, played baseball for Lake Forest College in Chicago. He was their pitcher, of all things. Sadly, I did not inherit his ability to throw a ball.

Being left brained, right-handed, and left-eyed and having to wear glasses for extreme near-sightedness probably conferred little advantage to me while I was engaged in sports! So, what to do? I certainly avoided physical fights because of my weight disadvantage. Although I was not the brightest bulb in the chandelier, I chose to pursue reading and academics in order to compensate for my lack of athletic prowess and capitalize on my strengths.

So, what did I read? I avoided the sports page for certain and to this day I cannot conceive of why some men only read the sports section of the newspaper and spend entire weekends watching an endless series of college and professional ball games.

This low-athletic trait probably made me a more favorable marriage candidate to my wife because she is about as athletic as I am. Actually, she is more athletic, because she likes to walk, stretches daily, and works out at the gym intermittently. Why, I ask, does she not lift our vacuum sweeper or cannot open food jars. She blames it on "poor upper body strength" since menopause. I could recommend some exercises, but probably won't, to keep the peace and ensure continuing marital harmony!

A sports fanatic I'm not, but I've been successful in my academic pursuits. I'm a decent cook, a good photographer, and I'm not a bad writer.

PETS I HAVE KNOWN

Although I had a goldfish and two hamsters during childhood, I think that nothing beats a cat or a dog as a pet. My two hamsters were named Mickey and Minnie, because of their mouse-like characteristics. So much for originality! I can't recall if my goldfish had a name. It's a real bummer to wake up one morning to find your pet hamster with rigor mortis or your goldfish floating belly-up in the water, so I switched to a dog.

Our first dog was a cocker spaniel named Sandy because of his blonde coat. He lived to about age five, but was silently spirited away to be euthanized by my mother when I was about eight. I suspect he had cancer, but to spirit away a pet without a word to an eight-year-old is just plain wrong.

Mother redeemed herself by taking me to pick out a new puppy, a miniature dachshund. I recall picking him because he was incredibly friendly, crawled into my arms, and began licking me immediately. We named him Fritz in honor of his German heritage. I enjoyed him for the next ten years. He routinely slept with me and I recall he would burrow under my covers for warmth and then come out when he got too hot. This process of burrowing in and out repeated itself over and over throughout the night. In the afternoon he would sit on his hind end on our sofa in front of our living room's picture window and patiently wait for me to return from school. He would always greet me with many kisses. He would routinely lick my ears, inside and out, keeping them spotlessly clean. We took him to Puerto Rico with us on a 707 jet and he got to sit with me in the passenger compartment. That was when the skies were friendly and the airlines were too. He returned to the states with us and lived with us on Silver Hills in New Albany until he was shot and killed by some neighborhood boys when I was a senior in high school.

Fritz

My parents replaced Fritz with Heini, a black dachshund, but since I was at college, he wasn't really my dog. Heini had a love-hate relationship with my mother. Although he was a loving dog, when she left for more than a few days, he would get angry and pee on her bedspread. So much for dachshunds!

It was only after many years that Mother told me the real reasons behind the deaths of Sandy and Fritz. I suppose she thought I was too young to understand Sandy's illness and death. As for Fritz, I think she was avoiding my possible reaction because she had let Fritz out and I had been quite angry with her when I returned from a trip to see Wabash College.

My next pet was a miniature schnauzer, another German breed. My first wife and I got him when I was a freshman in medical school because our neighbors Steve, also a medical student, and Linda had one and schnauzers seemed so friendly. Whiskers had a salt and pepper colored coat. My first wife and I enjoyed him immensely. He loved to go on walks. I recall that we went camping once and Whiskers immediately jumped out of our VW to inspect the campsite. Actually he did more than just inspect since he took it upon himself to precisely mark the edges of our 20-foot square campsite. How he knew the precise boundaries of that campsite in Yellowwood State Forest, I'll never know for certain, but I wonder if another dog had marked it and Whiskers smelled the boundaries. Sadly he died of kidney failure not long after my divorce.

Buster

My next dog was another miniature schnauzer, this time a black one. I named him Buster, my nickname used by my fiancée, Liz. Clever me, she couldn't use that nickname for me anymore!

I should have been wary because Buster was the last puppy left in the litter from a breeder near Turkey Run State Park. Moreover, I did not pick up on the warning sign of him biting his mother. He was able to wrest his way out of his box on the way home in my car, another warning sign.

Liz cleverly thought that we should buy a dog during our engagement so that I could housebreak him by the time she moved in after our wedding. Housebreaking was accomplished, but he bonded with me and was jealous of the attention that I gave her. When we sat on our "courting couch," he would worm his way between us. Building a barrier out of pillows and seat cushions was only partially successful, as he would usually find a way to circumvent this measure.

Buster proved to be a handful. He bit Liz as she attempted to correct him after he had chewed a hole in a hand-knit afghan, one of our wedding presents. When Buster was age three he bit our three-year-old nephew, John, in the face and that was the last straw! I took him to the vet to be neutered. Neutering fixed his aggressiveness, but he was none too happy about the loss of his gonads. On the way home from the vet he hugged the window by the passenger seat and would not even look at me. He knew what I had arranged for him. He lived to the ripe old age of 12 and died of age-related general deterioration.

A couple of years prior to Buster's demise, Liz was ready for a change, so she extracted a promise that we would get a cat. Our neighbors, Larry and Binny, had an American short-haired silver tabby with which we fell in love. He was a gorgeous cat who caused Liz and me to fall head-over-heals in love with silver tabbies. We went to a cat show at the Indiana State Fairgrounds and picked out Flash, so named because of his speed in escaping from Buster. He was four months old, the first of the litter to be sold, and was the pick of Janet, his local veterinarian breeder. Soon Flash and Buster became best friends and often slept cuddled up side-by-side on a step just outside our bedroom. They became such good friends that Flash stood vigil near Buster during the last two weeks of Buster's final illness. It was tender and moving to see such faithfulness.

After Buster was euthanized, Flash seemed lost in mourning, so we decided that he needed a playmate. We consulted our vet, Janet, and got an eight-week old female whom we named Felina. She was a cross between a silver tabby and a Scottish fold. Lonely Flash and tiny Felina who had just left her mother instantly became great friends. I remember that Flash was so loving that he would sit on my chest as I lay on the couch and repeatedly rub his nose on my forehead. Felina was more standoffish; she would only lie on my legs and face away from me.

Both Flash and Felina had a curious habit that I think was inbred. They would stand in front of their water bowl, repeatedly dip their front paws into the water, and then splash it on the floor or fling it across the room. Flash soaked the kitchen floor this way more than once.

Flash and Felina were three years apart in age and each lived to age 15, about average for this breed of indoor housecat. After Flash died of connective tissue cancer, Liz and I had Felina alone for three years, but she seemed lonely without a companion. After Felina became ill and was euthanized. Liz and I decided to wait a year to complete our mourning before getting another cat. However, we couldn't stand the emptiness of a house without a feline and acquired two more American short-haired silver tabbies. The first arrived within two months of Felina's death. Liz and I named him Sylvester, another original name!. About a year later Sophia arrived. They are good buddies who chase each other around our downstairs. First one pursues the other and then they switch and the pursuer becomes the pursued. It's incredibly funny! They have recently begun daily play fights which they put on for their owners' pleasure and entertainment. The World Wrestling Federation couldn't put on a better show! So ends the tale, or tails, of our dogs and cats.

Sophia (left) and Sylvester (right)

NICKNAMES

Like many of us, I have accumulated a number of nicknames over the years. Some are affectionate and some are not.

My mother never used nicknames with me. She always called me Phil or Philip. When she used my full name, "Philip Meredith Coons," I knew I was in trouble. That was usually followed by, "Wait until your father gets home." My father's affectionate nickname for me was "Bud."

My first nickname was "String Bean." I acquired this appellation because I was a very skinny kid and looked like a starving waif in a bathing suit. Goodness knows that my mother tried to fatten me up, but to no avail.

My second nickname was "Pot-Liquor." I acquired this nickname from one of my father's associates when I was 15. At first I thought it was "pot-licker" which I assumed to be derogatory as I imagined licking the bottom of a large black kettle. However, it was explained to me that pot-liquor was the best part left in the bottom of a pot after something had been cooked. I like to eat so that was an appealing nickname.

My next nickname was "the bod" which I acquired as a freshman in my college fraternity. At first I couldn't understand why I was called bod because I was still a skinny teenager. Then it dawned on me that my fraternity brothers were making fun of me. I wore this name with pride, however, and imagined that I really had a Bod, spelled with a capital B. My fraternity brothers also called me Coonsie or Coonie for obvious reasons.

As a young faculty member I acquired the nickname "Bone Doctor" from the nursing staff who had nicknamed my hyperactive anorexic patient "The Bionic Bone."

After I got married my wife Liz started calling me "Buster." She usually called be Buster when I had done something to aggravate her and it was a warning to "go no further." Liz eventually stopped calling me Buster, not because my behavior improved, but because we acquired a miniature schnauzer who I named Buster. This was one of my smarter moves, but, alas Buster died, and Liz picked up the habit of calling me Buster again.

Early in our marriage Liz also has called me Burt since she then admired the handsomeness of a younger Burt Reynolds. Sorry to disappoint you, dear, but I ain't no Burt Reynolds!

I picked up my last nickname in 2013 when I joined the Indianapolis Hiking Club. Another hiker nicknamed me "Paparazzi Phil" because I was always taking pictures of our hiking club adventures.

MUSIC

I love to listen to music of nearly all types but I can't read music or carry a tune in a bucket.

My first memory of making music was music class at School 84 in Indianapolis. I loved to bang on all types of percussion instruments. That was incredible fun.

My memories of music classes at Nora and Delaware Trail Grade Schools are few and far between. I do recall that we had to purchase tonettes, a plastic flute-like instrument. I could play the scale but that was the limit of my ability. When required to play a melody in a group, I confess I totally faked it. I still thank God that I was never required to play a solo. Looking back over my grades in music class in grade school I find that I made either As or Bs. Clearly my teacher wasn't paying close attention.

After I transferred to Westlane Junior High School in the sixth grade, our music teacher was Mr. Wheeler. What he taught was so far above my head that I was lost and I'm grateful that was the end of my formal music education.

My mother had played the violin in high school and my father had been in the orchestra in high school and had also taken voice lessons. Apparently his voice lessons didn't help much as his voice was far worse than mine. Since neither parent liked having to take music lessons, during childhood, neither my brother nor I were forced to do so.

My lack of musical ability has been well-noted in church. When we joined North United Methodist Church I was asked if I wanted to join the choir. I quickly responded that I could not sing and the subject was quickly dropped. Not so with a medical colleague of mine, an organist of immense capability. After a church service Mary Lynn looked at me with abject horror and announced, "You can't sing!" At Easter when we sing the Hallelujah Chorus, I often end a few bars behind, not that

I know precisely what a bar is! I think it is something we frequented as seniors at Wabash College.

I do appreciate good music. I love the Indianapolis Symphony and we often attend their concerts at Symphony on the Prairie at Conner Prairie Farm in the summer. My wife and I also had season tickets to the Indianapolis Opera for six or seven seasons.

I enjoy those who can sing and play an instrument but I am totally dumbfounded by how people can play. How in the world does one look at a sheet of music and then coordinate their fingers to play an instrument? I guess that is just one of life's great mysteries! No, it's not a mystery. I think we are definitely wired differently.

DANCING LESSONS

Nothing instills more terror into the heart of a fifth grade boy than the thought of taking dancing lessons.

Although my thoughts about having to take dance lessons at age eleven are now totally forgotten and possibly the victim of unconscious repression, I cannot conceive of having looked forward to such a possibility. I recall that my brother, four years older than I, preceded me at Mrs. Gates' Dancing School held at the Riviera Club in Indianapolis in the 1940s and 1950s.

I attended Mrs. Gates' Dancing School for two years with 75 other boys and girls. The dancing class was held in a large ballroom on the second floor of the main building at the Riviera Club. During our lessons the ballroom was ringed with chairs upon which all of us well-scrubbed kids sat. The dress code was exacting; boys wore coats and ties and girls wore dresses, hose, flats, and white gloves. Certainly no tennis shoes! How we sat was important; the girls were to sit demurely with their legs crossed at the ankles. We learned the waltz, foxtrot, cha-cha, and jitterbug.

Although I was too young to be interested in girls, I do remember one young lady in particular. Her name was Karen and she was fun to talk to so I often approached her and asked her to dance with me.

During my seventh and eighth grades about 25 of us kids in the Meridian Hills area banded together for more private dance lessons. I cannot recall where we met but it was probably someone's home or possibly a country club. Dress was more casual and we learned the popular dances.

I quickly forgot all of my dance moves except the basic box step for the waltz.

In high school I attended a number of dances, sock hops, and two proms. I loved to slow dance to such tunes as Paul Anka's "Put Your Head on My Shoulder," Pat Boone's "Love Letters in the Sand," and

"Venus" by Frankie Avalon. I was OK at the jitterbug and I learned how to do the twist. I never had the moves for the more free-style dancing and whenever I tried I looked like Ray Romano on "Everybody Loves Raymond." Somehow I made it through a number of blind dates in college by only asking my date for slow dances.

I made it through about ten years of marriage before my wife extracted a promise from me to take dancing lessons. She wanted lessons because she had been raised in a fundamentalist church where dancing had been prohibited. We chose to attend the Arthur Murray Dance Studio on the west side of Indianapolis on Lafayette Road.

I can still recall our first dance lesson. My wife Liz observed that I looked like a scared deer that had become frozen in the headlights of a rapidly approaching car. She was right; I was terrified and I remember looking out of the studio's big picture window and wishing that I could somehow dash out and escape to my comfortable couch at home.

To make long story short, we learned a number of dances including waltz, foxtrot, cha-cha, swing, hustle, rumba, and a few other Latin dances. We chose to concentrate on the hustle, swing, and rumba. I never could master the Cuban motion required of the Latin dances. Our dance instructor even took me to a private back room where she attempted with her hands on my hips to guide my recalcitrant derriere. However, it was to no avail.

Nowadays I've regressed to my former self. I still like to slow dance. Sometimes Liz can cajole me to the dance floor for a fast dance, but much to her chagrin, it has to be the hustle at just the right tempo.

CHAPTER 10

SPIRITUALITY

"I've been baptized three times, probably because I needed it."

MY THREE BAPTISMS

I've been baptized three times, probably because I needed it. I don't remember my first baptism which occurred on my first birthday according to my baby book lovingly kept by my mother. My initial baptism was delayed because my father, stationed in France after WWII ended, was awaiting the accumulation of enough points to be discharged home. He needed 85 and the 12 points awarded when I was born helped his total considerably. I was baptized at the First Presbyterian Church in Indianapolis by the Rev. George Arthur Franz, our family's beloved family minister for many years. At the baptism ceremony my cousin Greg was also baptized. He was three months old.

My second baptism occurred in 1980 at the Grace Brethren Church in Indianapolis. This baptism followed my being born again after a spiritual drought of 13 years. I was dunked three times forward and I can attest that the water was very cold.

I waited another eight years for my third baptism which was the most memorable. In 1988 Liz and I were vacationing in Peru and Bolivia. We had finished our tour of the ancient ruins of Machu Picchu and had taken the train across the Altiplano to Puno, Peru, which was on the edge of Lake Titicaca at an altitude of 12,500 feet. We boarded a boat to cross over into Bolivia. Once across the lake we took a small skiff to the *Isla del Sol* [Island of the Sun]. This island is believed to be the place where the Sun God Inti and the Moon Goddess, the primordial Adam and Eve of Incan mythology, originated.

Our guide Eduardo obtained branches from a sacred bush for our Inca baptism. As we floated quietly Eduardo dipped the bush branches into the lake's deep blue water and sprinkled us as we recited the three laws of the Incan empire in Quechua, the Indian language: "Don't lie, don't steal, and don't be lazy."

There you have it: two sprinklings and one dunking. Liz has drawn the line at her two baptisms which she thinks are quite enough, but I don't know!

SUNDAY SCHOOL

Danyelle, our children's pastor, had a bright idea for summertime Sunday school: Ask interested adults if they would be willing to demonstrate their greatest passion, talent, or hobby to the K-5 kids at North United Methodist Church. "Great, sign me up," I said, not having the foggiest notion of what I was getting into. I had previously taught adult Sunday school. "There couldn't be too much difference," I thought. Not having spent a lot of time around kindergarteners and kids in primary school, little did I know what awaited me.

I chose photography. Others chose toy trains, weaving, Spanish, quilt-making, etc.

The June day dawned bright and beautiful on this naive soul. I took my materials which consisted of several cameras, pictures of cameras that I'd owned since childhood, and pictures of different film types to the appointed classroom.

Several kids had already been dropped off by their parents. A Dutch door with a lock on it separated the classroom from the hallway. This should have been my first clue. A darling little blonde girl, about age four, with long pigtails was riding her six-year-old brother around the room horsey style. The only thing missing was a saddle and riding crop. "This is going to be fun," I unknowingly thought as I snapped a picture of this adorable scene.

More kids arrived. Soon the room erupted in pandemonium. I missed my second clue.

We did start at the appointed time. We sat on the floor in a semicircle with me at the front. I began my demonstration by talking about a Kodak box camera that I had used as a child. I passed around pictures of the camera and black and white roll film. Prior to talking about my second camera, a Kodak Brownie, the class had to be shushed. "Clap once if you can hear me," a matron shouted above the din. They clapped but nothing happened. Boisterousness at about 80-90 decibels continued unabated. "Clap twice if you can hear me," the matron shouted again. This time they clapped and quieted down. "What a wonderful technique this is that my child psychiatry professors never taught me," I thought. We talked a little more about cameras and film, but soon the kids were as loud as ever. "Clap once if you can hear me. Clap twice if you can hear me. Clap three times if you can hear me," and the room quieted down again. The matron also separated two male friends who were misbehaving. "Another trick my child psychiatry professors had failed to teach me!

With classroom instruction at an end, I proceeded with my plans to do a lab practical. We divided the group into thirds. The older kids went with my wife and an adult helper to take pictures outside. I figured correctly that with two adults, these kids could get into little trouble. The youngest kids stayed in the room behind the locked Dutch door. They were safe from harm. I took the intermediate-aged kids to the sanctuary to take pictures.

My group of five boys was barely out the door before they screamed with glee and ran pell-mell down the hall. Pandemonium had erupted again and I was on my own! Struggling to keep up, I followed them to the sanctuary. No sooner than had they arrived in the sanctuary, they split up. One boy hid under a pew and wouldn't come out. Another two raced towards the front, removed the microphone, and began chattering loudly. I don't know where the other two were because my peripheral eyesight could not cover the great expanse of the sanctuary. One boy had my camera and began taking pictures. I finally was able to wrest it from his control so another boy could take some pictures of his own. The horseplay continued.

When it was finally time to return to the classroom, I corralled three of them, but where were the other two? Thinking that they had fled to the street and been run over, my worst fear, I led the three I had hold of back to the classroom and locked them in. My wife brought her group back. Then, lo and behold, the two missing boys reappeared. My frantic prayers had been answered.

Class ended. I left, shaking with pent-up anxiety, on the arms of my wife. We sat in our pew. I calmed down, but can recall nothing of that Sunday's service.

When I got home, I downloaded the photos from the three cameras. The kids from all three groups had taken some great shots. There were some out-of-focus shots that I had to delete too. I posted our pictures on our church's website.

What one little ruffian in my group didn't know was that he had activated the movie setting on my camera. I had a perfect record of what had transpired in the sanctuary. I haven't shown anyone this clip, so the guilty are known only to God and me!

GOD TALK

I was raised in the Presbyterian Church. Baptized as an infant in the First Presbyterian Church in Indianapolis, Indiana, I attended there until age 14 and then St John's Presbyterian Church in New Albany after my family moved there when I was age 16.

I have some foggy memories of First Presbyterian. We were taught some Bible stories in Sunday school as small children and then in about the fourth or fifth grade we were supposed to memorize the books of the Old and New Testaments. This was a turn-off for me since I am not good at memorization. However, some of the girls in Sunday school were excellent at memorizing and could recite the Old Testament books lickety-split. Later, I married a woman who could rattle off the twelve Old Testament minor prophets in five seconds, but that's another story.

Another turnoff for me was the term "Holy Ghost." This concept of the Holy Spirit or the third persona in the Christian Trinity was never adequately explained. We boys thought it was a real ghost, something out of the horror movies perhaps, something to fear, or something to make light of in dealing with our fear.

As I recall there was an undue focus on the Apostle Paul at both First Presbyterian and St. John's. I could never understand why there was so much emphasis on the problems with the early Christian church and very little emphasis on Jesus, the founder of the Christian church. Although we had a youth group at St. John's, it couldn't hold a candle to the Methodist Youth Fellowship as I have experienced it in later years.

I also recall the *Time Magazine* cover for April 8, 1966. Blazoned across the front of the magazine in bold letters was the question, "Is God Dead.?" Apparently God had died that year and I had been caught totally unaware, as no one, including this dead God, had bothered to inform me.

So much for my early church upbringing! Let's look at how I came to understand, God, Jesus, and the Holy Spirit.

As a fourth grade student at Delaware Trails Elementary School we studied astronomy in science. I can well remember going out to my backyard, looking through a telescope, and being amazed at the sight of the stars and the visible planets. At this moment I knew that there had to be a God to create our amazing universe. This belief has only strengthened during the past 60 years as more and more of our marvelous universe has been revealed through radio telescopes and the amazing Hubble Telescope.

When I attended the Indiana University Geologic Field Station in Montana during the summer of my junior year in high school I marveled at the age of the earth, 4.5 billion years old. "Wow," I thought! "What had God wrought?"

In Introductory Biology at Wabash College I marveled at the amazing construction of the one-celled organism called Euglena. Here was a flagellated protozoan, an animal, containing chlorophyll. Here is a marvelous creation, a cross between an animal and a plant. Then we studied evolution, the real way that I think God used to create humankind. Amazing! Only God could have done this. I concluded that the creation of the earth, our natural world, and all of its amazing plant and animal life, could not have been created by chance collisions among molecules. Science opened my eyes to the Creator.

As a medical student I continued to marvel at the wonder of the human body. What an amazing engineering feat! So now I understand why Martin Luther King, Jr., said that it is illogical to not believe in God after observing our natural world and the heavens beyond.

Now what about Jesus? After my divorce at age 35 I began to learn more about this guy, first at Tabernacle Presbyterian Church and then in Jim and Barb's Bible study which I attended for a couple of years via Tabernacle. At last I had found a Presbyterian Church that knew something about Jesus. I also had a couple of friends, Ed, a hospital chaplain, and Liz, a medical student, who kindly answered my questions. I became "born again." I actually saw the face of Jesus in a person. Was this a hallucination, an illusion, my imagination, a religious experience, or what? I don't know for sure, but I know I met Jesus, and he changed my life.

What an amazing guy, this Jesus was! Although my wife and I left the Presbyterian Church in 1985 and became Methodists, I've continued learning about Jesus over the years, primarily through some of our Sunday school offerings at North United Methodist Church in Indianapolis. I've read some of the non-canonical gospels and studied some of the books by John Crossan, a free-thinking Catholic priest, and Philip Gully, a Quaker pastor, both of whom have been highly criticized by conservative Christians. Crossan even had his life threatened by some so-called "Christians." At any rate, I'd have to describe my thinking about Jesus as being highly liberal at this point, but his admonition to "Love one another," is central to my religious beliefs. Although I try very hard to follow Jesus, I suspect that I fail considerably in my efforts. I take solace in the knowledge that I am "saved by grace," a decidedly orthodox idea. My wife says there is such a thing as a liberal evangelical. If that's true, it's what I am.

What about the Holy Spirit? My admonition to Sunday school teachers is to lose the term, "Holy Ghost," as it tends to be totally confusing to both children and adults. My simpleton belief is that the Holy Spirit is God within us and God surrounding us. That belief developed after I joined North United Methodist Church and observed and felt the Spirit freely moving into, out of, and all around us. I can't explain it. The power of the Holy Spirit can only be felt and experienced, whether it be through thunderous organ music, beautiful choral music, prayer, caring for a dying member of a Sunday school class, or participating in service projects such as the Appalachian Service Project (more about that later).

There you have it, my religious and spiritual beliefs. They continue to develop. The adventure continues!

APPALACHIA SERVICE PROJECT

In 1969 the Rev. Glenn "Tex" Evans, a Methodist minister, started the Appalachia Service Project (ASP) in Kentucky. He and a group of fifty teens and adult volunteers helped repair four homes in the Barbourville, Kentucky area. Since that time 44 years ago, 300,000 volunteers have helped make 15,000 homes in Appalachia "dryer, safer, and warmer." Home repair might involve re-roofing, insulating, applying siding, putting up wall board, and remodeling kitchens and bathrooms. Currently the ASP works in five states: Kentucky, Tennessee, West Virginia, Virginia, and North Carolina.

During the last three years it has been my privilege to accompany youth and adult volunteers from North United Methodist Church in Indianapolis, Indiana on their annual journey to Kentucky to volunteer with the ASP. We have worked in Harlan ("Bloody Harlan"), Breathitt, and Leslie Counties in Kentucky.

ASP week is more than just a week of service. We sign up for the experience nearly a full year in advance. We contribute about $350 each to participate and that amount is just half of the cost. Our congregation contributes the other half. Our main expense is renting the vans which transport five youth and two volunteers each to Kentucky and back again. One van rental alone costs about $1000 each with another $200 for gasoline.

In preparation for our week of service we have several organizational meetings and two "practice builds" where we work on a small project in the Indianapolis area. Then, on the Saturday before we leave, we "pack and load" our vans. The next day, Sunday, we arrive at church at 6:30 AM, have a small breakfast provided by church volunteers, and then we're off to Kentucky.

We usually arrive at the ASP center in our assigned county by about 2:30 PM, unload our vans, and get settled. After orientation by our college-student staff we have dinner, and then it is off to our worksites to meet our families and reconnoiter our repair projects.

The centers where we stay deserve a special word. They usually are elementary schools and the sleeping quarters are generally on the floors of individual classrooms. We, of course, bring sleeping bags and air mattresses upon which to rest our weary bods at night. Bathroom facilities are usually Spartan or built for grade schoolers. Showers are usually constructed outside and the water is usually cold. During my first year, we used outdoor privies and the teens showered in the "coal room" of the school. We may or may not have air conditioning.

Each morning Monday through Friday during our work week we get up at 7 AM, have morning devotions at 7:30, and eat breakfast at 8:00. Then we prepare our lunches, usually PB&J sandwiches, load our vans with materials from the daily hardware store runs, and start off to our worksites by about 9:00.

One of the most rewarding things about the ASP experience is getting to know our families. These families range from young couples with little children, to middle-aged couples, to single adults. They are nearly all severely impoverished. Many are disabled or infirm from old age. Many are unemployed and few have had the privilege of much education.

Nearly all of our work sites have animals of various kinds. Dogs are the most numerous, but there are cats, chickens, roosters, and pet raccoons. During my second year one family had fighting cocks which they raised and sold for illegal fights. I suppose some families make moonshine. We don't ask and don't tell! Oh yes, there are snakes and spiders at our work sites.

At about 4:30 PM we return to the ASP center where we are staying, take showers, and have some free time before dinner at 6:00 PM. During the evenings we have short programs. On Wednesday nights we have "culture night" which might involve listening to a bluegrass band. On Thursday evenings we and our families have an outdoor picnic at a local park. On Friday evenings we have a "sharing circle" during which we tell one another where we experienced God that week.

With the exception of spending times with our families, our sharing circles are one of my favorite parts of the ASP experience. The first year

I saw God in a newly married couple for whom we worked. At the end of our week they provided a wonderful barbeque dinner for us in their local church. That same year an old man brought us a huge jug of cold water from a spring near his house. The second year God woke me in the middle of the night and told me that I had to buy a $350 table saw after the center's power saw had given up the ghost. We needed this saw so badly because we needed hundreds of spindles for our stair and railing projects. This year I saw God in the little children at one of our sites. I also saw God in the adult volunteers, nearly all of whom had given up a week's vacation to go and do hard manual volunteer work without pay.

When I described to my Sunday school the horrible ASP facility that we stayed in my first year and the horrible heat and humidity, I was asked incredulously, "Are you going to do this next year?" Yes," I said, "in a heartbeat." Nothing about the physical discomfort of our lodging accommodations came close to the spiritual thrill of helping poor families live with comforts that I've taken for granted my entire life.

CHAPTER 11

FAMILY

"The driveway leading to [my grandmother Coons' farm] was gravel and was lined with tall narrow poplar trees. A tall wide hedge just off the highway shielded view of the house from passersby. A variety of hardwoods dotted the property and cherry, peach, and apple trees grew in a small orchard in back of the house. Kitty had a large cut flower garden and also a vegetable garden of about half an acre. The entrance to the garden was framed by a large grape arbor. Outbuildings included a large barn painted green, a storage shed, chicken coop, and a still functioning one-holer outhouse."

MOTHER

My mother, Margaret Richman Coons, was born in Columbus, Indiana on November 13, 1913 to Frank and Edith Rogers Richman. She had an older brother, Philip, and two younger sisters, Frances and Elizabeth. Her father was an attorney and later an Indiana Supreme Court justice. Their family home was on Riverside Drive in Columbus.

During her high school years at Columbus Central she was on the newspaper and yearbook staffs, played the violin, and was a member of the scholastic honor society. She attended DePauw University for one year and was a member of Kappa Kappa Gamma sorority. As a sophomore, her father transferred her to Indiana University where she graduated with a degree in Latin.

Although she worked as a librarian prior to marriage, she was a full-time homemaker afterwards. She was a great cook. Her passions included reading, working crossword puzzles, gardening, and travel. She traveled throughout the United States and numerous foreign countries in Europe and Asia.

Among my fondest memories of Mother are those from when I was in high school and Steve was away at college, I would sit in the kitchen on a tall bar stool as Mother was preparing dinner. Dad was always late in getting home from work, so it was just the two of us. Unlike a lot of other young men my age, I would tell her about my day and discuss school, current events, and my current love life. Our discussions were sometimes spirited, but always respectful. It was a way of establishing my identity, I think.

My mother, Margaret R. Coons

Mother was a reluctant grandmother and preferred to be called Grand-Marge rather than Grandma. She was a nervous great grandmother, especially when her great granddaughters (Lori Coons O'Connor's children), Kelly and Kasey Jo, came to visit and merrily skipped over her oxygen line, and their brother Jack tried to climb the fireplace equipment.

Mother had many directions for me, her son. These directions included the usual "Mom-isms": make your bed, pick up your toys, go to Sunday school, and get a haircut. The last time I heard her instruction to get a haircut was when Dad and I had just returned from a three-week trip to Europe in the summer of 1980. She picked us up at the airport in Louisville, Kentucky. It was dusk and the light was low, and as I was getting in the backseat of the car, without looking around she said, "Phil, get a haircut." The problem was that I had just had a haircut at the Frankfort, Germany airport literally eight hours previously. She was just doing what mothers do everywhere!

We seldom ate chicken at our house and I think I know why. When she was about six, she and her family had just returned home from an automobile trip. After alighting from the car, she was scared by a chicken which she thought was chasing her. She was so scared that she ran around the block, thinking all the while that the chicken was close on her heels. That experience engendered a life-long fear of birds so we had no pet parakeets and she comically ducked and cowered whenever a songbird swooped in low over her head while she was gardening. In spite of her fears she loved to feed and watch the birds, from a distance and separated by a pane of window glass.

Mother loved her dogs. As a child she had a black mutt named Duke and while I was growing up we had a succession of dogs, including Sandy, Fritz, and Heini. But we had no cats. I'm not certain where she developed her dislike of cats, but by the time I arrived, her dislike was full-blown. I remember when I was a child on Sherwood Drive in Indianapolis she would garden in our backyard. Our next-door neighbors, the Trusty family, had a rather large tomcat named Davy Crocket. That cat would take great delight in emerging from the fencerow separating our properties and pouncing unannounced into the middle of whatever she was tending. He was her nemesis. I remember that when Liz and I got our first two cats, Flash and Felina, I had them in a cage when she came to visit. "Mother," I said, "Do you want me to get the cats out so that you can see them closely?" "Absolutely not," she replied.

So, even though I infrequently ate chicken as a child and had no pet kittens, I was not deprived. My life was incredibly enriched through her presence and influence. She died at age 84 of emphysema, and my life has been poorer because her absence in it. She was truly a loving and wonderful woman.

MOMISMS

My mother had numerous sayings, but they were not made up on the spot, nor were they sexualized like by father's sayings. I've often wondered if there was a book or pamphlet for mothers containing these sayings because all the mothers of my peers said essentially the same things. Did Dr. Spock write about these? Did mothers get together behind our backs and plot to say these things? Mothers are the main socializers of their sons, because, Goodness knows, fathers aren't. Here are a few of my mother's favorite sayings:

1. Because I said so, that's why.
2. Because I'm your mother.
3. Wait till your father gets home.
4. Don't go out without your hat and coat, or you'll catch your death of cold.
5. No dessert if you don't clean your plate.
6. Clean your plate. Think of the starving Armenians.
7. You need a haircut.
8. Clean your room.
9. Make your bed.
10. Yes, you have to go to church.
11. Is your homework done yet?
12. Don't tease the dog.
13. Don't chew with your mouth open.
14. Don't sass me, or I'll wash your moth out with soap!
15. Just wait till you have your own children.
16. If I have to stop this car, we're turning around and going home.
17. If I've said it once, I've said it a thousand times.
18. You're not going out of the house wearing that.
19. It's time to get up.
20. Wash behind your ears.

21. Shut the door. We don't live in a barn.
22. Sit up straight.
23. Wipe that smile off your face, mister.
24. If you cross your eyes, they'll get stuck that way.
25. I don't care what other parents say.
26. And my all-time favorite, Kissing leads to things.

All in all, my mother's Momisms served me well, despite my irritation with them.

DAD

Dad was born on July 31, 2011 at home in New Market, Indiana. His father, Merle, had AB and master's degrees from Wabash College in Crawfordsville, Indiana. Merle Coons was a school teacher, principal, and school superintendent of the Montgomery County, Indiana schools until he was elected to the Indiana House of Representatives where he served from 1934 to 1940. Dad's mother, Clara Leona Van Cleave, attended DePauw University and served five terms in the Indiana House of Representatives between 1941 and 1957. Both of Dad's parents sold school textbooks in Indiana for the Webster Publishing Company in St. Louis.

Like his father, Dad graduated from Wabash College and went on to Indiana University School of Law in Bloomington, Indiana. While attending IU Dad met and courted my mother. After graduating from law school, he went back to Crawfordsville where he opened a law practice. Since it was the middle of the Great Depression, business was slow to nonexistent, so Dad began working for the Aetna Insurance Company as an insurance claims adjustor.

When WWII intervened, Dad was drafted into the Army in late 1943, even though he was married with a two and a half year old son, Steve, at the time. After basic training at Fort Bragg, North Carolina and Camp Rucker, Alabama, Dad was sent to France in December, 1944. He was assigned to the field artillery in the 66th Division and helped guard a German submarine base in the *L'orient* sector of Brittany. Following the cessation of hostilities in France, Dad's unit moved first to Baumholder, Germany and later to Marseilles in southern France. He ended his tour of duty by working in the Criminal Investigation Division in Paris and came home in April, 1946.

Upon his return from WWII Dad joined a partnership in an insurance adjusting firm in Indianapolis where we lived until I was age 14. At that time Dad's partner had a brain tumor and was unable to work. Although Dad valiantly strived to support both our family and his partner's family for nearly a year, his efforts couldn't succeed indefinitely, so the business was sold and we moved to Puerto Rico when I was 14, where Dad was an officer in a low-cost housing project. This business venture did not succeed, however, so our family moved back to Indiana, where Dad became a partner in another insurance adjusting firm in New Albany. He remained in New Albany until his death in 1999. During that time he served several terms as Republican County Chairman and one partial term as a Floyd County Circuit Court judge.

My father, Harold Coons

What I remember most about Dad was our family vacations together. Early on we vacationed at Big Star Lake in Michigan and Lake Tippecanoe in Kosciusko County, Indiana. During the winter holidays between school terms we would often go to Florida where we spent many memorable times at Bradenton Beach and Sanibel Island. When I was age twelve, Mother, Dad, and I traveled the Blue Ridge Parkway in North Carolina and Virginia. We went to Old Williamsburg and ended up in Washington, DC, our final destination. In 1980 Dad and I went to Europe for three weeks and visited many sites where he had been stationed during WWII.

Dad was a loving, generous, and highly principled man. In addition to his generosity to his insurance adjusting partner's family, Dad was highly ethical and fair to a fault. Once when an employee stole from him, instead of filing charges, Dad arranged restitution and all was forgiven.

Dad's love and concern for my mother was touching to observe. He served as her caretaker during the final stages of emphysema that ultimately took her life. He took superb care of mother, even though he too was suffering from emphysema which would finally take his life a year and a half later. My dad was a real inspiration to me which I will never forget. I'll always admire him.

DADISMS

My father and first father-in-law were well-known for making up sayings, some quotable and some not so quotable so I hesitate repeating them here, but I will anyway. Edward, my second father-in-law, bless his heart, was a Grace Brethren minister and never behaved as badly as the other two. A little naive, he once when at our house announced after reading the TV section of the newspaper that he was planning to watch "Midnight Cowboy." Almost in unison my wife and I cried out, "That's not a western, Dad."

My father's dadisms:

> A master at giving a teenager double messages he said, "Don't give her a corsage. Give her a massage," or, "You don't need to buy a cow to get a little milk." He followed both sayings up with "But keep your pants zipped up, Bud."

> He had a slightly sarcastic bent: "Love makes the world go around" and "Ain't love grand?"

> When consoling me over being dumped by a girlfriend or rejected for a date he would pronounce, "Women are like street cars. One comes along every ten minutes." I couldn't appreciate his advice at the time.

> At dinner time when passing the rolls he would chirp, "Do you want a roll or do you want to wrestle?"

Bob, my first father-in-law's dadisms:

> After drinking a stiff martini he would say, "Let's all get naked and jump in a pile."

> On getting gasoline and relieving oneself on long auto trips, "Take a little and leave a little."

> Forever an optimist and a bit egotistical he would pronounce, "It's hard to be humble when you are as great as I am."

> Always clean and well-dressed, he mowed his yard after work in a white dress shirt. "If you can't be pretty, at least you can be clean," he would declare.

> In contrast, my mother and Mildred, my wife's mother, offered some really sage advice:

> "Kissing leads to things," they both said, and it did!

STEVIE

As a little tyke my brother Stephen was known as "Stevie," and referred to himself as "Tee-Tee" until he could pronounce his *ST*s. Even before I was born Stevie had endeared himself to my parents via his antics, of which I will describe several.

My dad had left for WWII Army service on February 9, 1944. While Dad was gone my mother and brother lived intermittently with her parents in Columbus, Indiana. It was there that Stevie pulled off a couple of wing-dingers. Somehow this almost three-year-old was able to maneuver his grandmother Richman's tea wagon from the house to the porch. His next stunt was to begin painting their garage door. When confronted by my grandmother about what grandfather Richman was going to say, Stevie quipped, "My, my, how fine, how fine. Tee-Tee painted the garage."

During the fall of 1944 Mother and Stevie moved to Ozark, Alabama to be closer to my father who was stationed at Camp Rucker. Housing was scarce, but Mother finally found a small house to rent. While the landlady and Mother were discussing terms, three-year-old Stevie felt the urge to pee, which he did off the side of the porch. Mother felt for certain that she had lost the house, but the landlady took pity on her and rented her the house anyway.

Two hilarious things happened with Stevie while Dad was overseas. First President Roosevelt died in April, 1945. Mother notified her cousin June, who was living nearby, and that evening June and her son John came over for dinner. According to my mother, Stevie and John went wild, putting green beans in each other's milk, liberally peppering their food, and spreading margarine all over their plates. The next morning Stevie, playing Paul Revere, was up early, out the door, and announcing, "President Roosevelt died yesterday." Then in late April, Mother got the premature news from a neighbor that Germany had surrendered. Mother had been giving Stevie a bath, and when he heard the news, he jumped out of the bathtub, ran out of the cottage without a stitch of clothing, and announced to everyone within hearing range, "The war is over! The war is over!" It took Mother fifteen minutes to catch the naked little devil.

Eventually I came along in mid-1945 about eight months after Dad had left for Europe. I swear that I can recall Stevie tearing along sandy Bradenton Beach, Florida. He was pushing a baby carriage with me in it, and I was scared! Although I was still an infant, sibling rivalry had kicked in, and I'm convinced Stevie was trying to get rid of me! A picture of this is in our family archives.

Stevie pushing me in a baby carriage on Bradenton Beach

During those early years sibling rivalry persisted. When we went somewhere in the car, Steve and I were consigned to the back seat. Like many siblings, we fought over who owned the center of the back seat. Eventually my parents tired of this and bought a foreign car, a Jaguar, which had an armrest in the middle of the back seat. My parents thought, "Problem solved," but no, it wasn't, because we fought over who owned the middle of the armrest!

KITTY

My grandmother Coons derived her nickname from my brother Steve who named her Kitty because of all the cats on her farm. That was good enough for me, so when I arrived and began to speak, that nickname stuck.

Of all my grandparents Kitty was my out-and-out favorite and the reason was not hard to discern because she spoiled her two grandsons rotten. I must admit that her farm helped because of all its attractions to this city boy. The other reason that I built such a strong bond with her was her fabulous cooking.

Kitty's cooking could be described as old-fashioned, Midwest county cooking. A few of my favorite dishes were her fried chicken, mashed potatoes and gravy, fresh green beans, corn on the cob, applesauce, and tomatoes fresh from the garden. Kitty was an expert at baking cakes and pies and she also made homemade ice cream. Yummy! Her hash-brown potatoes were delectable. Several times she made pressed chicken sandwiches for my date and I to take on a picnic. Fortunately, I inherited her *Joy of Cooking* cookbook so I have been able to recreate several of my favorite dishes.

Kitty

The lure of her farm and fabulous cooking were not all that attracted me to Kitty. She was the most loving grandmother a child could want. I remember when I was little and my brother and I were visiting her farm, we would get up early in the morning and crawl into her feather bed, one of us on either side of her. While we cuddled with her under her heavy quilts, she would tell us stories. What these stories were about I've long since forgotten, but I have not forgotten the warmness of her loving embrace.

Kitty was quite talented. In addition to being a great cook, she could sing and play the piano, a grand piano which sat in her living room. She was a talented gardener who raised all kinds of flowers, fruits and vegetables. For example, her gladioli and peony blossoms were stupendous. She was a talented artist and during late adolescence had enrolled in art classes at DePauw University. She painted at least five oil paintings of landscapes and still-life flower scenes. Later in life she became a skilled ceramicist, creating colorful and humorous pieces, including a purple milk cow stepping on her teat.

Prior to her marriage she taught art in the New Richmond and Wingate public school systems. After her marriage she reared one son, my father, and then began working for the Webster Publishing Company selling school books all over the state of Indiana. After her husband Merle died, she continued working for Webster and also served five terms in the Indiana House of Representatives in 1941, 1943, 1945, 1947, and 1957. I recall proudly serving as her legislative page for a day when I was 12 or 13.

When I attended Wabash College, Kitty was always there for me. She regularly did my laundry and had me over for dinner on many Sundays during the school terms. When I had a date over for a weekend dance at Wabash, she housed my date and the date of another fraternity brother. This made it easier to get a weekend date.

Kitty was a talented seamstress who made many articles of clothing for both herself and her family. She made some of her own curtains. I recall that when she visited us in Puerto Rico during Christmas, 1959 she had made our pet miniature dachshund a Christmas outfit consisting of hat and coat.

Sadly I lost Kitty to cancer in July, 1967 barely two months after I had graduated from Wabash College. Although she has departed this earth, she will always be in my memory. She provided a host of warm memories of my youth. I was truly blest to have Kitty as my grandmother.

KITTY'S FARM

My grandmother Clara "Kitty" Coons lived on a farm just off Indiana 47 about seven miles south of Crawfordsville, Indiana. After the death of my grandfather, Merle, in 1940, she moved from their home on Market Street in Crawfordsville and remodeled an old home on the farm that she owned. This was a real working farm operated by a tenant farmer who lived on the airport road just east of Kitty's house. The farm surrounded the house on three sides and extended east for some distance to her tenant's home.

The driveway leading to her home was gravel and was lined with tall narrow poplar trees. A tall wide hedge just off the highway shielded view of the house from passersby. A variety of hardwoods dotted the property and cherry, peach, and apple trees grew in a small orchard in back of the house. Kitty had a large cut flower garden and also a vegetable garden of about half an acre. The entrance to the garden was framed by a large grape arbor. Outbuildings included a large barn painted green, a storage shed, chicken coop, and a still functioning one-holer outhouse.

Kitty's farmhouse and barn

Kitty's garden provided our family and her friends with an abundance of fresh produce. She canned peaches and made cherry pies and apple sauce. In the summer we always had an abundance of green beans, sweet corn, lettuce, radishes, and potatoes. In the late spring we feasted on her home-grown strawberries which were also frozen for winter use. Kitty even grew popcorn which she brought to us unshelled in large five-gallon cans.

Her home was two stories with two bedrooms upstairs, one of which was unheated, and a large attic just under the eaves. Downstairs was a kitchen, huge living room lined with built-in bookcases, a third bedroom, a bathroom, and a large dining room with beautiful cherry paneling extending downward from a chair-rail. A window seat with large picture window looked east from the dining room. A utility room just off the dining room contained the furnace and water-heater.

Outside the kitchen and dining room was a brick patio and close to the kitchen door was a large cistern and pump from which Kitty hand pumped soft water for cooking and bathing. Behind the garage was a windmill which pumped well water for both the house and watering the livestock of pigs and cows.

A large breezeway connected the house with a large two-car garage. The breezeway, which was entirely screened-in, was a cool summertime haunt for family and guests. It contained an abundance of white-painted wicker furniture including a rocking couch, two rocking chairs, footstools, and side-tables.

In the early 1950s Kitty built an unheated concrete block utility house beside the patio. This small building contained a large chest freezer in which she kept an abundance of meat, fruits, and vegetables frozen for winter consumption. It also contained a kiln which she used for her ceramic-making hobby.

On the farm lived an abundance of sparrows which often produced loud chirping music during the summer. Besides the usual cows and pigs, Kitty used to keep a few chickens which provided fresh eggs. There always seemed to be plenty of barn cats which were dumped on the farm by city dwellers who perhaps knew that my grandmother had a soft spot in her heart for cats and fed them regularly. The cats rounded out their diet the plentitude of mice they caught in the barn. Squirrels and chipmunks were few and far between owing to the presence of the cats.

GRANDMA AND GRANDPA RICHMAN

My grandparents on my mother's side were Frank and Edith Rogers Richman. They moved to Indianapolis from Columbus, Indiana in the late 1940s and lived just off Central Avenue on East 53rd Street. Their house was small with just two bedrooms upstairs but they were empty-nesters. Their postage-stamp sized yard could be easily mowed with a push-type reel mower.

Grandfather Richman was an attorney from Columbus, Indiana. From 1940 to 1947 he served as a justice on the Indiana Supreme Court. In 1947 he and Edith traveled to Nuremburg, Germany where he represented the United States as a justice in the Flick Trial. They returned from Germany in 1948 just after the trial because Edith had been involved in a severe auto accident while sightseeing. She required a transfusion of plasma and developed hepatitis from it. This was discovered on her voyage home to America. From 1947 to 1952 Frank was a Professor at the Indiana University School of Law in Indianapolis. After he retired he served twice as Judge-Pro-Tem for the Fayette County, Indiana Circuit Court. Sadly he died of colon cancer in 1956.

Frank N. Richman

I have only a few memories of Grandpa. He smoked a pipe and I loved the smell of his pipe tobacco, so much so that I bought a pipe when I entered college. To my huge chagrin I found that smoking a pipe was not as pleasant as smelling pipe tobacco while someone else smokes. I also recall taking several Thanksgiving Day walks in the nearby woods of Marott Park with Grandpa after we had eaten our fill at our home on Sherwood Drive.

The best description of Grandma Richman is that she was very reserved. She was thin, a wisp of a woman and for as long as I knew her she had white hair, not just streaks of white, but totally white. I think she had grey hair when she delivered her last child, my Aunt Beth. Perhaps delivering a last child at age 44 is enough to give anyone grey hair. I recall that Grandma playing the piano and her living room was filled with figurines that she and Grandpa had acquired in Germany in 1947 and on subsequent visits.

Edith R. Richman

I remember that when we ate at Grandma's house it was always in the dining room and the table was always set formally. That's where I learned the use of all the different forks and spoons. I don't rest on formality now. You usually get one knife, one fork, and one spoon when I prepare dinner.

The salad that I remember best that Grandmother served was tomato aspic. On a number of occasions Grandma served beef tongue which she considered a delicacy; I did not!

Grandma Richman died of primary liver cancer in 1968, almost one year after I had lost Grandmother Coons (Kitty). Losing two grandmothers about a year apart was not an auspicious way to start medical school. However, I shall never forget the indelible lesson that serum hepatitis can result in liver cancer years later.

EXTENDED RICHMAN FAMILY

My mother, Margaret Richman Coons, and her siblings were all reared in Columbus, Indiana. After the children married, they situated themselves in four different states: my parents in Indiana, Aunt Frances and her family in Oklahoma, Uncle Phil and his family in Virginia, and Aunt Beth and her family in California.

It's fascinating to reflect upon how far geographically this one family has spread and to think about the myriad of occupations which their descendants and spouses possess. If my count is correct, the Frank and Edith Richman descendants have resided in 15 different states: California, Colorado, Florida, Georgia, Idaho, Indiana, Maryland, Massachusetts, New Hampshire, New York, North Carolina, Oklahoma, Oregon, Texas, and Virginia.

Their occupations have been even more diverse. Amongst the original Richman siblings and their spouses were three attorneys, two school teachers, and three homemakers. Of their nine children and their spouses there are two psychiatrists, an airline pilot, a wedding planner, an attorney, a playwright, a business journalist, a nurse, two IBM employees, a Ball Corp engineer who worked on the Hubble telescope, an artist, and several who worked in various occupations including construction, logging, and mining.

The fourth generation descendants and spouses present an even wider array of occupations. They include an economist who works for the census bureau, a professor of economics, a private investigator and Army reservist, a book publisher, an entrepreneur, a sales representative, a non-profit specialist, several homemakers, a song writer and performer, a world traveler and blogger, a locksmith, and a computer programmer.

Of the fifth generation who knows where Sam, Benjamin, Evangeline, Samuel, Jake, Hawk, Piper, Nash, Cole, Elizabeth, John, Joshua, Gracelyn, Hartley, Abigail, Ben and the as yet unborn will live or what their occupations will be?

SPITFIRE

I didn't intentionally set out to marry a spitfire, but that's what happened. Liz and I met in a mental hospital, and it always startles people when we tell them that. It makes for good conversation at a cocktail party.

As a junior medical student, Liz was on my inpatient team at Larue Carter Hospital when I was just beginning my career. After her rotation we stayed in touch periodically and after my divorce we began to have a few meals together and became good friends. During my fall 1980 trip to Europe with my father, we both noticed how much we missed one another and after my return we decided to start dating. We fell in love and married the following September.

Liz had a couple of conditions for marriage. One was that I learn to put the toilet seat down. She even utilized a little behavior modification by placing a sticky note on the underside of toilet lid to remind me. It worked and I'm certain it preserved our future marital harmony. The second condition was that I replace our house's ancient kitchen sink which had a kinky hard-to-use faucet and was growing mold in its porcelain recesses. This task was not easy as I couldn't afford to hire a professional. So I did it myself and I don't still know how! I replaced the sink, water faucets, disposal, and countertop and even installed a tile splashboard. I was in love, and still am.

Liz is smart as a whip, my intellectual superior for sure. She's a quick wit and has a comeback no matter what I say. I like that. It keeps me from becoming too full of myself. She told me that she used to sharpen her tongue by bantering with her male boss when she was in college.

We have a lot of shared interests such as travel, the outdoors, and photography. We are in accord spiritually and politically. We share vocational interests since we are both physicians and we've written a number of publications together including a book on the history of psychiatry in Indiana. Liz's editing skills have been a Godsend for me and you can bet she's editing this one. Our families are compatible. We enjoy each other's friends and are good friends ourselves.

The stories I could tell, but won't, since she's editing my memoir! But here are a couple that are printable that won't get me in the doghouse.

The first two episodes occurred after we were first married. In the first episode in our first month of marriage I was driving up our driveway after a long day at work and I thought Liz was waving "hello," so I rolled down my car window and discovered she was screaming and waving her arms because she couldn't get open the screen door which had a tricky lock. After a rapid repair, marital harmony was restored. In the second episode in our 1930's home I had just flushed a toilet downstairs when Liz appeared at the top of the stairs stark naked. As she rushed downstairs towards me screaming all the way, I realized she wasn't in the mood for conjugal relations! She had been showering and the water had suddenly turned burning hot. She likes a hot-water shower, but not scalding. The temporary fix for that problem was simple: don't flush the toilet when the wife is in the shower. The permanent solution was purchasing a newer house

At this writing we've been married 32 years. We've been through a lot, but each crisis has brought us closer together. These crises have included the loss of three parents and Liz's cancer. Would I marry Liz again? In a heartbeat!

SAYING GOODBYE

Both of my parents died of emphysema, many years after they had started smoking. Mother died at age 84 and Dad at age 88. Had they not smoked, each could have added about seven years to their lifespans. Both of their families had many individuals who lived into their 90s.

I first noticed Mother short of breath when my parents and I visited Switzerland in 1979 with a Wabash College alumni group. Mother was finding it difficult to get to the top of a short hill where her condo was. I eventually noticed Dad getting short of breath about five years later as he was sawing a log with an electric chain saw on the hill behind their house in New Albany.

Mother was the first to quit smoking after I suggested pulmonary function tests when I was a sophomore in medical school. Her sister Frances had also been on her case to quit. As many know, there's nothing worse than an ex-smoker, so Dad was exiled to the garage or outdoors to smoke. Dad eventually quit smoking, or so we thought. After he died in 1999 my brother and I heard that he had continued sneaking cigarettes despite his steadily worsening emphysema and being on home oxygen.

As their pulmonary functions steadily deteriorated, my parents both started seeing a pulmonologist in New Albany. My mother told me that she had heard that dying from emphysema was an easy death. "You just go to sleep and never wake up," she said, not knowing the misery that I had observed at my local Veteran's Hospital, not to mention the "chartomegaly," or huge medical charts that these poor emphysematous vets accumulated.

Mother was the first to go on home oxygen, initially provided by an oxygen "concentrator." She was tethered to this contraption 24-7. She was a real trooper, however, and dutifully did her walking exercises at home in New Albany and during winters in their condo in Fort Myers Beach, Florida. I recall that as my parents' pulmonary function deteriorated, they found it difficult to make beds alone, even a single bed, so they worked in tandem, one on each side of the bed, huffing and puffing.

About one and a half years prior to Mother's death, she and Dad visited the Canadian Rockies. Something happened out there and Mother was admitted to the hospital almost as soon as she returned home to New Albany. She almost died the night of admission with my brother spending the entire night at her bedside. She pulled through somehow, but was never quite the same mentally. She became severely depressed, probably due to the steroids that she was taking for her emphysema. Closing the drapes to her bedroom and refusing to come out or take nourishment, she wanted to die. "Phil, can I die if I take all of my medicine?" she asked. She had one of the most severe depressions that I had ever seen outside of a psychiatric ward. I started her on a tiny dose of an antidepressant medication and over about seven or ten days her depression lifted. I think this medication saved her from suicide.

My niece Caroline moved in to help care for her. My brother and I became my parent's meals-on-wheels, because the service of the same name would not deliver meals to their upscale New Albany neighborhood. Steve flew in from Atlanta and I drove to New Albany from Indianapolis.

Although all was not peaches and cream, neither was life totally depressing. The power went out during a thunderstorm late that summer. Mother was alone at home at the time. Sensing danger, since her oxygen concentrator had quit functioning, she walked uphill one block to the head of the street for help when she saw an electric utility truck at the intersection of Highland Avenue and Riddle Road. That must have been a herculean effort for her. I was astounded when I heard what she had done. I'm sure she must have felt desperate.

I vividly recall sitting outside on my parent's porch one crisp fall day. I was reading medical records which I had brought with me to New Albany. It was warm and the sun was shining. The sky was a brilliant blue. Mother came to the door, opened it a bit, and gave me one of those smiles that only a mother can give. Her loving smile made me feel warm inside. I smile when I remember that moment.

Despite our best efforts, however, Dad could not cope with Mother's declining health. He finally arranged for her care in a local nursing home in Clarksville, about ten miles from their home in New Albany. Years before both Mother and Dad had earnestly promised one other that they would not ever send one another to a nursing home. I recall the tears in Dad's eyes when he finally made the decision. He was broken up and it was exceedingly painful for me to watch, but we both knew it was the most loving thing he could have done for her.

Eventually Dad moved into an independent living apartment in the same facility because he was becoming worn out just driving between home and the nursing home in Clarksville. Again this was something Dad had promised himself he would never do. "I'll never leave my home. They'll have to carry me out of my house feet first."

Mother lived for about another six months after graduating from six months in a hospice program. Her end came after she caught the flu from a visitor or employee. The flu became pneumonia and she was admitted to the hospital where she died in a couple of weeks. "I can save you," her physician said, but she bravely declined any heroic life-saving measures, just like her father had in his final days. Clearly, this was the best move for her because she had been in stage-four respiratory failure, or short of breath at rest, ever since entering the nursing home.

She was clear-headed to the end. I recall her asking me on one of my visits to the hospital whether President Clinton had bought Monica Lewinsky a Cadillac. I guess that idea had come from the television that had been on in her room. "No, Mother. I don't think so," I said, trying to stifle my snicker.

Mother died on a cold day in early February 1998. I had just left New Albany to return to Indianapolis. The next day I returned to New Albany in a heavy snowstorm. At her funeral both Steve and I gave eulogies, while Dad sat forlorn in the front row at their church. We buried her in Columbus, Indiana at City Cemetery, next to her parents. I recall that Steve and I trudged through the few inches of snow on the ground as we carried her burial urn to its final resting place. That was a sad day.

After Mother died in 1998 Dad thought he would like to start visiting friends and relatives around the United States, but he was prevented from doing so by his lung condition. . He had also stopped attending the Wabash College class agents' meetings in Crawfordsville for the same reason. For him not attend these meetings must have been a painful decision, because he was the ever-loyal alum and had been a class agent for many years. My brother and I did drive with him to and from his condo in Florida one more time and I'll never forget that trip.

I had planned to drive the entire way, but who did I see in the driver's seat when I returned from a filling station restroom in middle Tennessee? It was Old Dad! We were off, but in Florida he set the auto-pilot to 85 miles an hour despite the frequent construction zones, many of which had empty squad cars parked in the median. At one point we were coming up fast on a slow car and he didn't know what to do. "Dad, put your foot on the brake" I yelled, scared out of my mind. I warned my brother, so his return trip from Florida with Dad was uneventful.

Dad eventually went on home oxygen and my visits to New Albany became more frequent, from once every two weeks, to twice a week at the end. Like Mother, he was on an antidepressant medication. "Happy Pappy pills," he called them. On my visits I did his laundry and went to the grocery. By this time the grocery list was mercifully short since he was on Ensure liquid supplements and had lunch and dinner provided by the retirement center. He had occasional accidents with loose stools which I cleaned up. Now our roles had completely reversed. I was the parent and caretaker and he was the child. It was grueling work and lonely being away from Liz, but there was a sad satisfaction to caring for my faithfully loving father.

Dad's condition continued to deteriorate. He ordered a motorized wheelchair. Finally one day I arrived at his apartment for my visit and I discovered him lying across his bed with only his shorts on. He had been unable to get out of bed that morning. I helped him dress, we went to his doctor's office, and he was speedily admitted to the hospital. A chest x-ray was taken that I reviewed myself. There was some density at the bases of his lungs, but I couldn't tell if it was a pulmonary effusion (fluid on the lungs) or pneumonia. I went to say goodbye and said that I'd see him the next morning so we could consult together with his physician. That was the last time I saw him alive. In the morning at about 5 AM I received a call from the hospital nurse that he was dead. I was stunned and couldn't believe it. He apparently had gotten up, intending to shave, but had fallen and badly bruised his forehead.

We had the funeral, and again both my brother and I gave eulogies. Another sad trip to the Columbus City Cemetery! This time the weather was better, a beautiful September day.

I'll never forget my parents. I couldn't have done better if I'd picked them myself. Once, maybe ten years before Dad died, he asked me if he'd been a good father. He was worried that he hadn't spent enough time with me due to his busy hard-working schedule. Without hesitation and knowing that he had provided me with a college education and continued tuition help through medical school, I earnestly said that he had.

CHAPTER 12

LIZ'S CANCER

"When we arose the next morning, she had projectile vomiting and I knew that I had to take her to the hospital. Something was seriously wrong inside her brain. She was suffering from the effects of increased cerebral pressure."

THE WORST DAY OF OUR LIVES

I had been vaguely aware that something was wrong. Since I had known her, Liz had always run a low blood pressure. On occasion she would get out of bed or get up from a seated posture, feel lightheaded, and have to steady herself to keep from falling. It was getting worse, however. When she attended a professional meeting, she lost her balance during a vertiginous episode and nearly fell to the floor in the corridor just outside her hotel room.

Shortly thereafter when we went to Rick's Boatyard Restaurant for dinner, I had to support her during another vertiginous episode as we emerged from the restaurant on our way to the car. I almost took her to the hospital that evening, but she was fine when we got home. On our way to the car, I thought of Annette Funichello. An unsteadiness of gait is how her multiple sclerosis first manifested itself. Curiously, I noticed that Liz began to sleep later than usual after she had returned from her psychiatric meeting.

The following week, however, was a different story. One night, as we were watching a movie video, she had a brief headache lasting less than a couple of minutes. When I looked at her eyes she had nystagmus [horizontal eye movements, first rapidly in one direction and then more slowly in the opposite direction.]

It was then that she told me that she had been having very brief headaches and associated dizziness lasting two or three minutes for several months. She had dismissed these headaches as stress-related and hadn't told me.

The next night, she was awakened with a brief severe headache. The night after that, she had both a headache and vomited. When we arose the next morning, she had projectile vomiting and I knew that I had to take her to the hospital. Something was seriously wrong inside her brain. She was suffering from the effects of increased cerebral pressure.

I told Liz that I was taking her to the hospital and that no objections could deter me from my mission. First I called a friend and colleague in the Indiana University School of Medicine Neurology Department. She happened to be a headache specialist, although I had a suspicion that this was not a benign headache case. She listened sympathetically and with much concern and suggested that she would call the neurology resident on call while we made our way to the hospital admitting/emergency room.

We had a short wait before a neurology resident arrived, took Liz's history, and performed one of the most comprehensive neurological examinations that I had ever witnessed. Her examination was mostly normal except that she had nystagmus, an abnormal reflex in her left foot, and diminished sensation in both her left arm and leg. In the middle of her examination, she had an episode of nystagmus and retching. When the resident had finished, we discussed that Liz's symptoms could be due to a variety of conditions including migraine headaches, multiple sclerosis, or what she and I expected, a dreaded brain tumor. Her symptoms were confusing and did not point to a definitive diagnosis. What was indicated, however, was a brain MRI (magnetic resonance imaging).

After an extended wait for the MRI tech on call to arrive, we were escorted back to the MRI suite. Ordinarily, family members wait in a separate waiting room, but this was a holiday. There were only three of us in MRI: Liz, our MRI tech, and me. I waited for what seemed like an eternity, surely the longest hour in my life. The banging of the MRI machine was nerve-racking enough for me. I couldn't imagine how it was for Liz. I paced back and forth.

The MRI suite had glass partitions or windows. The outer room, where I was waiting, had a glass window looking into a control room where the MRI tech was sitting. On the opposite side of the control room was another glass window, through which we could both see Liz lying with her head and chest in a massive tube. The MRI tech was facing Liz and the MRI machine; her back was towards me. Several times, I surreptitiously looked at her computer monitor as she was receiving numerous MRI images. A series of images caught my eye. Even from 10-12 feet away from the computer screen I could see that there was a mass in the right frontal area of her brain. I was shocked to the very depth of my being. As a physician I had seen MRI images of brain tumors and this one was relatively large.

Liz emerged from the MRI suite and we sat down again in the patient examination room. I didn't say anything to Liz about what I had seen. I was hoping against hope that the images were of someone else, perhaps the last patient before Liz to have had a head MRI. I saw our resident pass by the room. He averted his gaze as he passed by and I knew. Pretty soon both the he and his supervising staff physician, arrived with the bad news. The four of us walked down the hall to view her MRI images. As soon as Liz saw the images, she almost slumped to the floor from emotional shock and I had to hold her up as we walked back to the exam room.

Arrangements were made for immediate admission. An IV was started and Liz received the first of many injections of steroids to decrease the swelling of her brain. This provided immediate relief from her nausea and vomiting which had continued episodically all morning and afternoon.

After Liz was situated in her room, I began the first of many telephone calls to notify our family and friends and to cancel her week's schedule of patients.

So ended the worst day of our lives and sound sleep for both of us for many nights to come.

THE DAY OF SURGERY

The day of surgery is one that I would rather forget altogether. I arose early and made it to the hospital at about 7:00 AM. Liz's surgery was not scheduled until early afternoon. She had a number of tests that morning including a final MRI and neuropsychological testing. Somehow she found time to undergo hypnosis with a psychiatric resident to enhance control of operative bleeding and post-operative pain and nausea. She had a steady stream of visitors and flower deliveries all morning.

Shortly after noon I accompanied Liz to the operating room suite and we said our goodbyes. Then I did something that still astounds me. I knew that I couldn't sit still in the surgical family waiting area for a four or five-hour surgery. I also knew that our lawn needed mowing, so I raced home, put on my grubbies, and literally tore around the yard pushing my lawnmower in a mad frenzy. I showered and was back to the hospital within an hour and a half. I had been told that the preparation for the actual surgery would take about an hour and I knew from experience that by the time I returned the surgeons would be just about to cut through the dura mater covering her brain. I made it back in plenty of time and was in the waiting area a full hour before the first report came from the operating room.

During my long wait in the surgical waiting area, a number of friends and family dropped by to sit with me. I really appreciated the comfort they offered.

It was not easy sitting in the waiting area. Midway through Liz's surgery a surgeon came out and talked to an elderly woman sitting right next to me. His words were not comforting. Her husband had an abdominal cancer and it has spread throughout his abdomen.

Finally it was my turn to talk to our surgeon. He arrived just after finishing surgery. He had both good news and bad. Liz had survived the surgery, and he had removed 98% of the tumor, but the tumor looked cancerous and highly malignant. If it was what he thought it was, Liz had a 50-50 chance of surviving a year. He tried to remain hopeful responding to my question about recurrence. He had several patients who had second or even third surgeries and they lived longer than a year. I was devastated, but this was merely a confirmation of what I had feared from the first day of hospitalization.

In about an hour, I was summoned to the recovery room. When I arrived, Liz was just awakening from anesthesia. She was asked who she was. She knew her name and I thought, "By golly. That's good. She knows her name." Then she was asked, "Do you know where you are?" She said, "Sure, we're in the surgical recovery room. I used to do electroconvulsive therapy over there," as she pointed to a corner of the room. At that moment I knew that she was not brain damaged, although she would have a long road to recovery.

A little later I followed Liz up to the sterile-looking neurosurgical intensive care unit. She was hooked up to numerous wires and tubes. We kissed good night and I began a long drive home.

AT FIRST YOU CRY, AND CRY, AND CRY, AND CRY SOME MORE

Liz and I cried when she was told of her diagnosis and poor prognosis. We cried before surgery. We cried after surgery. We cried on the day she received her official tissue diagnosis. We cried with each other. We cried alone. We cried with friends and family.

Bad news brought tears. The sight of family and friends brought tears. Get-well cards brought tears. Flowers brought tears. The experience of kind acts brought tears.

Sometimes I would cry and Liz wouldn't. Sometimes she cried and I wouldn't. Sometimes we cried together. We always held one another while we cried.

Nearly anything could trigger tears which would come on suddenly and without warning. Sometimes one or the other of us would avoid crying because it was just too painful.

The crying continued off and on, off and on, and off and on for months and months.

As Liz's tumor receded from treatment we gained some hope. We cried less often, but the worry and sadness inside us lingered until an MRI found no tumor. Then the tears were those of joy, relief, and gratitude.

FAMILY AND FRIENDS

Neither Liz nor I would have survived her cancer ordeal very successfully had it not been for the support of our family and friends. Their kind support started the first day of hospitalization when I telephoned some of our closest friends and it continued over the months to follow.

It's hard to imagine the number of get-well cards and e-mails we received, let alone their kind and comforting messages. Liz was comforted and her hope was sparked by this outpouring of good wishes.

Several early encounters with joyful kindness typify the incredible support that Liz and I received. The first occurred just after Liz had returned from the neurosurgical intensive care unit. A half-hearted attempt had been made by Liz's nurses to clean her hair of Betadine disinfectant and glue from electroencephalographic leads. Her hair, however, was still a mess of clotted blood. Laura, one of Liz's colleagues was visiting and helped shampoo Liz's hair and comb out the cruddy tangles of filthy hair. The sight of this ultimate act of motherly kindness made me cry. A day or so later, Inna, a neighbor physician and immigrant from Armenia, gave Liz a therapeutic massage to relieve her pain and tension. After she arrived home, one of her best friends, Jennifer, arrived after driving seven hours from Missouri. She stayed for a week, cooked, cleaned, and cried with us. She brought us great comfort. Jim, one of Liz's colleagues, flew in from Boston to say goodbye to her.

Subsequently, we had numerous visits from friends, many of whom brought food including their best versions of chicken soup. There were numerous special family recipes. I can't describe all of the salads, vegetables, fruits, meat dishes, and deserts that we received.

Our families were equally supportive. My brother Steve visited us daily when Liz was in the hospital. He treated his tired, stressed brother to dinner on several occasions when Liz was hospitalized. Liz's brother Phil, sister-in-law Dawn, and two of their children, John and Brittany, came to visit during the month of July and then returned again just after Christmas.

Liz received numerous bouquets of flowers during her hospitalization. By the time she left the hospital, her two-room suite could have passed for a flower shop. We took two carts of flowers home with us and left numerous bouquets for the nurses. After we arrived home, flowers continued to arrive. The same delivery woman brought many bouquets to our house and finally remarked to Liz, "You must have a lot of friends."

The cards, visits, flours, and invitations for lunches continued for months and months. At time the visits were overwhelming, especially during her hospitalization and in her immediate post-hospital course. A crudely lettered sign on the hospital room door told visitors when the shop was closed for business. Later Liz had to place a moratorium on invitations for lunches. It wasn't that she didn't appreciate the offers or desire to be with her friends, but with such frequent invitations she couldn't accomplish her everyday tasks at home and at work.

Probably the most touching experience occurred when Liz and I went to visit Jennifer and her pastor husband John in Missouri. On Sunday morning we went to church. At the end of the concerns section, John invited us to the alter where the elders held a laying-on-of-hands for healing. While we knelt they laid their hands on her and a special choir sang a lovely song with the refrain, "We are praying for you." I couldn't stop crying. Then we knelt before the alter and John said a prayer of healing. We were both so moved and many in the congregation were crying. They had been praying for us for months.

THE WELLNESS COMMUNITY

If there was one thing that has enabled both Liz and me to cope with her horrible cancer, it was the Wellness Community (now known as the Cancer Support Community). Indianapolis is blessed to have this resource. Currently the Cancer Support Community has 47 sites in 25 states and has affiliates and partners in seven countries. The Cancer Support Community offers support groups to cancer patients and their family members in addition to transitional grief groups for family members who have attended support groups prior to the deaths of their loved ones. There is no cost for this service since it is totally supported by corporate and individual donors.

I told Liz the other day that somehow we might have muddled through without our groups, but both of us felt our support groups had been invaluable. In the beginning, it was the education. Initially we attended three workshops about radiation therapy, fatigue, and brain tumors. As time went on, the group enabled me to express thoughts and feelings about what was happening to me and us. It deepened our communication and in our groups we were able to express the unsaid, the forbidden, the horror, and the joy. We were able to make financial arrangements, talk about death, cry together, tell each other how much we loved one another, and plan Liz's funeral.

Dealing with cancer is a roller coaster of emotions with intense highs and intense lows. The lows, of course, are associated with bad news. The highs come with good news, hope, and support of friends and family. I think the highs and lows are accentuated by the support group. It's not easy talking about painful subjects and more pain is inflicted in the process. However, I missed group when I had to be away. While away from the group my feelings were muted. I usually didn't hurt, but I didn't feel intense joy either. I simply avoided myself.

During one group our facilitator, shared with us what attracted her to work at the Wellness Community. She knew nothing about the Wellness Community, but had been approached by a client who inquired about cancer groups. In true social worker fashion she set out to inform herself, located the office of the Wellness Community, and came to learn more. Before long she was going to workshops, volunteering, and when a position became vacant there, she closed her private practice and took it. She felt that it was a privilege working with us. For her it was very much unlike traditional psychotherapy.

One of my group members was Don, whose daughter Deb had the same kind of brain cancer that Liz had, a glioblastoma. Deb was diagnosed four months before Liz, had surgery and then radiation. She was re-operated eight months later for a rapidly growing recurrence. Like Liz, her tumor had been in her frontal lobe, but unlike Liz's tumor, was on the same side as her speech center. The initial surgery affected her speech some and her speech worsened as the tumor regrew. Her speech worsened again with the second surgery. Her memory problems were much worse than Liz's occasional minor difficulties. Deb was able to drive after the initial surgery, but at times got lost, and would have to call her family on her cell phone. Deb began to have seizures after the second surgery and her driving was curtailed altogether.

Deb was an amazing person. She was a champion swimmer who had garnered many awards. She had a swimmer's physique and had dark hair and expressive dark eyes. Even after her second surgery she continued to swim under the watchful eye of a friend. Deb's family was amazing. She had an identical twin and a host of other siblings in a blended family. Her extended family filled up the waiting room during her second surgery. On her numerous forays to Duke University and the National Cancer Institute she was usually accompanied by several family members.

Liz and I followed in Deb's and Don's footsteps by four months. My greatest fear was that Liz's glioblastoma would be as aggressive as Deb's. When Don talked in group, I was riveted in horror.

Deb died a few months after her second surgery and I fully expected that Liz would follow in her footsteps by about four months.

CANCER DREAMS

For several years after Liz's diagnosis with brain cancer we both had dreams about the cancer. Freud called some of these dreams anxiety dreams.

Here is one of my anxiety dreams which occurred seven months after her initial diagnosis:

> I had a dream about Liz's cancer. This time we were passengers in a car being driven quite rapidly on a gravel road up and down razor-edged ridges lined with trees. In the distance we could see a large granite dome much like the domes found east of Atlanta, Georgia or in the Australian outback (Ayers Rock). Neither of us has been to either one but we expected to visit both someday. At the end of the dream we plunged down a ridge to a straight strip of road where we slowed down and lost sight of the granite dome, our ultimate destination. I am quite convinced that the dome represented Liz's death from cancer which had been well within sight. The wild up-and-down ride represented our roller-coaster feelings in dealing with the cancer. The slowing down onto a straight stretch of road and loss of sight of the "dome" represented favorable news from Liz's most recent MRI.

A second dream is what Freud called a wish-fulfillment dream:

> I had a dream about Liz's cancer. I was in a huge tree with a single large branch upon which I stood. Lodged in the branch was a large wedge-shaped growth. I was leaning against the trunk and with all my might I was jumping up and down on the branch trying to dislodge

the growth. After much effort, it finally fell to the ground and with a giant thud it raised a cloud of dust. Was this a futile wish for a cure or a message from God that Liz is healed?

I no longer have dreams about her cancer although I'm still somewhat anxious if she exhibits a symptom which reminds me of her original cancer symptoms.

Is Liz cured? We've been told that this cancer can never be cured, but it certainly is in remission and she and I have the fervent hope that it stays in remission for many years to come.

A TOUCHING SCENE

Liz and I went to Crawfordsville, Indiana to visit my cousin Autumn, who was in her late 90s and was in a local nursing home following surgical fixation of a fractured hip. She was tiny, weighing in at only 103 pounds, and had severely deformed arthritic hands. She had the sweetest smile and her mind was extremely sharp. She read two newspapers a day and always retained what she had read months previously.

Liz and Autumn really loved and admired one another. Autumn always asked about Liz when I visited alone. Liz had told Autumn about her brain tumor in a previous phone conversation.

On our visit we talked about various things, but Liz and Autumn mostly focused on coping with their respective illnesses. There was a very strong connection between them. As we were preparing to leave, Liz and Autumn grasped one another's forearms, young smooth muscular arms grasping thin wrinkled arms ending in almost useless hands. They smiled widely at each other and looked deeply into each other's eyes and Liz said, "We are both fighters aren't we?" Autumn agreed as they held their grasp. One could almost see the energy and strength as it flowed from one to the other.

I felt so privileged to have viewed this touching scene between women of two far removed and vastly different generations. Here were an old woman, who personally knew Civil War veterans, and a woman half her age who was born nearly 100 years after that war had ended. Autumn had been a music teacher, farmwife, and homemaker and Liz was a physician and medical school professor living a life that women of Autumn's generation could only dream about. Despite the generations that separated them, this was a timeless and sacred woman to woman connection.

CHAPTER 13

LIFE CHANGING EXPERIENCES

"When I finished my stint in the path lab at the end of the summer, I was crowned 'Urine King' and given a small cake with flaming candles on top. It was a fun party, but a dubious honor."

PUERTO RICO

My parents and I lived in Puerto Rico during my freshman year in high school. Due to the illness of my father's business partner, they had sold their independent insurance adjusting business and Dad embarked on a new career as an officer in a low-cost housing business in Puerto Rico.

Our family flew to Miami just after school let out in June, 1959. From Miami we flew to San Juan. I can still remember sitting by the window in a 707 jet watching the many hues of blue and green water as we coursed over the Bahama Islands. I also recall stepping onto the flight stairs and going down to the airport tarmac. I felt a sense of mild disorientation in the bright sunlight as I realized that there really were lands outside of the continental United States and over the ocean waters, as I had read in the *National Geographic*.

Our first days of living in a fourth floor penthouse in an apartment building on Calle Esteban Gonzalez in Rio Piedras, a southern suburb of San Juan, were hectic. Our furniture would not arrive for several more weeks. I slept in my own bedroom on a large board topped by an air mattress, all of which rested between two large glass blocks. It took my mother an entire day of going to seven different government bureaus to obtain her Puerto Rican driver's license. When our old refrigerator finally arrived, it took several workmen three hours to finally get it into our apartment. In the end they had to remove the refrigerator door to get it around one stair landing. Of course, once situated in the kitchen, it would not start, so several more days were required to repair and that included an additional trip up and down four flights of stairs.

Our Buick arrived on the same boat as our furniture, necessitating visits to several more government bureaus and the payment of a large import tax to get it properly registered. Not long after the Buick arrived, the engine on Dad's MG sedan exploded. A repair shop had to completely dismantle the engine to get it repaired. I remember looking on in horror at the engine completely disassembled on the repair shop floor. To my surprise and relief the mechanic finally got it back together after several weeks.

One thing we learned about Puerto Rican culture was the concept of *mañana*. Nothing ever happens until *mañana*, an unspecified time in the future. This was a tough concept to learn for a non-Hispanic OC family, who expected for everything to happen on time.

Our family spent the summer going to various beaches, getting sunburned, and visiting various tourist sites such as the fort [*La Fottaleza*] El Morro, Old [*Viejo*] San Juan, and the rain forest on *El Yunke*, a 2300-foot mountain in Puerto Rico's lush Luquillo Mountains. Eventually Dad was able to procure a membership in the Reserve Officer's Club near Old San Juan. It contained a place to eat and a marvelous beach reached by descending stairs down a cliff, so we frequented this beach often.

When fall arrived I started the ninth grade at St. John's Preparatory School in Santurce, another San Juan suburb. I remember going to a few parties at the home of Joaquin and Cinca's, our Puerto Rican friends who were anxious to introduce us to Puerto Rican culture and food. I'll never forget trying chitlins (cooked intestines of a pig) for the first and only time. I discretely spit them into a napkin. I also ate my first and only hot pepper. It burned both coming and going, but I'll spare the gentle reader the details of the latter experience. I drank a lot of water that evening. I can't believe I ate the whole thing, but I didn't know any better. The party lasted until 4:30 in the morning but our exhausted family made it till only 2:30 when we left just prior to desert being served.

My brother Steve, who was a freshman at Wabash College in Indiana, arrived for Christmas break along with my grandmother Kitty. We had a good time that Christmas and even had a miniature Christmas tree set on a table. It felt strange celebrating Christmas in a warm climate. After about a month Kitty returned to the states with a longtime friend, Gladys Leslie, wife of former Indiana governor Harry Leslie. Instead of flying back, Kitty and Gladys took a slow freighter on which they had booked a stateroom.

During my spring break, my grade school chum, Lee, flew down for a visit. In addition to seeing all of the tourist sites, one day we flew in a drafty DC3 over to the island of St. Thomas. We did the usual touristy things such as go to the beach, explore Charlotte Amalie, and take a taxi to Crown Mountain, the highest point on the island. This was a neat adventure and the first time I had traveled without my parents.

By the end of the school year, it was clear that the low-cost housing venture that my father was working for was going to fail so we packed our bags and returned to the states. We spent the summer in a rental home in Riviera Beach, Florida, giving Dad time to sort through his employment options. In the end he decided to become a partner in an independent insurance adjusting firm in New Albany, Indiana. This firm eventually became known as Coons and Horton where Dad worked until he retired and went into politics and the practice of law.

Sadly I did not become fluent in Spanish during my year in Puerto Rico. Although my first year of Spanish in high school provided me with a solid background, I was too shy to try out my Spanish on the native Puerto Ricans.

THE PATHOLOGY LAB

My first job was working in the pathology laboratory at Floyd County Memorial Hospital in New Albany, Indiana. I began working there the summer after my sophomore year in high school and continued there for one or two more summers. I made minimum wage, which was $1.25 an hour. During the mornings I performed urinalyses and complete blood counts and during the afternoons I washed glassware. I won't describe some of the urines I tested, but "disgusting" is the best word I can conceive. Whenever anything went wrong with the chemistries the next day, it was always due to the "dirty glassware" and I always got a disapproving look from the lab-tech in charge.

Because I knew I wanted to be a physician, I often spent my lunch hour watching one of our three pathologists cut tissue for microscopic slides on whatever the surgeons had removed that morning. I saw lots of breasts, uteri, ovaries, appendices, gallbags, and whatever else the surgeons could think of to remove, primarily from women. I also observed a fair number of autopsies and recall having to sit down on the floor with my head between my knees after becoming faint from the stench of my first autopsy. I can still remember Della, our path tech coming in one morning after checking the morgue. "There's three of 'em in there," she said. "Let's go. I gotta see this," I said, full of excitement and anticipation." It was my first observation of multiple murder and murder-suicide.

My two and a half months in the path lab was a life-changing experience for me, not only because it cemented my desire to become a physician, but because it was my first job and it was also the first time that I had worked primarily with women, several of whom were of color. I think it was in the path lab that I first began to become a feminist.

These coworkers, which included Della, Fanny, Fran, Margaret, Mary Helen, Dr. N, and Dr. S., were fun to be around. We told dirty jokes, new to my virgin ears. Della taught be how to walk like a pimp.

We were often regaled with a description of the previous night's date with her fiancé by our lab secretary. The older married women were always sure to offer their earthy and sage advice.

When I finished my stint in the path lab at the end of the summer, I was crowned "Urine King" and given a small cake with flaming candles on top. It was a fun party, but a dubious honor.

It was a memorable summer. During future summers I learned how to cut tissue sections for staining and microscopic examination. This was a skill which I used in a senior biology project during my years at Wabash College, a project which prepared me for my histology course in medical school.

Those were the days.

INDIANA UNIVERSITY GEOLOGIC FIELD STATION: A LIFE CHANGING EXPERIENCE

In the summer of 1962, between my junior and senior years in high school, I was awarded a scholarship from the National Science Foundation to attend the Indiana University Geologic Field Station in the Tobacco Root Mountains near Cardwell in southwestern Montana. I was one of eight high school students, seven young men and one young woman, from across the nation to be awarded this privilege.

Now known as the Judson Mead Geologic Field Station, this facility was subsequently named in honor of Judson Mead, Ph.D., director of the field station from 1961 to 1981. The field station offered its first course in 1949 when Dr. Charles Deiss, the first director of the field station, selected the South Boulder Valley in the heart of the Tobacco Root Mountains because this region offered more varied geologic phenomena than any other area in the United States."

When I attended in 1962, the field station consisted of a lodge, serving as a library, lecture room, and dining hall, and a number of steel buildings, which functioned as male and female bunkhouses, shower facilities, laundry room, and research facilities. The male high school students were housed in four-man platform tents, which could become quite cold at night. A pond, nicknamed Lake Mead, was situated between the upper and lower campuses and often during the early evening beavers could be heard loudly slapping their tails on its water.

Indiana University Geologic Field Station, 1962

During my time at the field station the main course given to undergraduate college students was G429, an intense summer-long experience in field geology. At the time, a number of undergraduate and graduate students, who were working on various projects, were also in attendance. Students came from all over the United States and from several foreign countries. In 1962, in addition to students from Indiana University, G429 students came from 21 other universities around the United States. Eight of the students were women.

Our experience began in Bloomington, Indiana where we boarded "carryalls," a crossover between our modern vans and SUVs. Each vehicle carried about seven persons. Our vehicles were painted dark green and emblazoned with the Indiana University Geologic Field Station logo. All were equipped with two-way radios so that instructors could communicate with everyone in the convoy, thereby enhancing the teaching experience enroute. Along the way we studied our guidebooks which had been specially prepared for the trip.

We must have been a funny sight crossing the prairies from Illinois to South Dakota. Our course began with nearly a one-week trip from

Bloomington, Indiana to the field station in Montana. Along the way we visited such impressive geologic sites as the Black Hills in South Dakota, Wyoming's Devils Tower, the Big Horn and Bear Tooth mountains, and the Yellowstone and Grand Teton National Parks in Wyoming, and Hegbgen and Quake Lakes in Montana. During the middle of the summer we made trips to Butte, Montana to visit the copper mines and Glacier National Park in northwest Montana.

I was age 17 and this was my first trip west of the Wabash River in Indiana. It's hard to describe the emotional response I had when I first saw the snow-capped Rocky Mountains somewhere in Wyoming. I was amazed, exhilarated, awestruck, and humbled by their beauty.

We worked hard at the field station and often put in 18-hour days between arising and retiring. I bought a straw cowboy hat to keep the sun off my head and began to grow a mustache and beard. It was there I first learned how to do my own laundry. Once and only once I put starch in my blue jeans which turned out stiff as a board. I mistakenly thought starch belonged in all loads of laundry. While at the field camp I followed the G429 students around for the first couple of weeks and then helped several graduate students on their research projects. Although we worked immensely hard, it was a delightful summer full of interesting experiences.

On Saturday nights we high school students went into Whitehall to see a movie, while those over 21 went to the local watering holes. We had Sundays off and on these days we often went hiking or jeep-riding in the mountains. At this remote outpost we had no access to television or the newspapers so we rarely knew what was going on in the world.

At the end of our summer in Montana, four of us high school students hatched an idea to go to the Seattle World's Fair. We got permission from our parents and our big adventure was on. We stayed at the downtown Seattle YMCA, rode the monorail, went up in the Space Needle, went to many science exhibits, and enjoyed several plays including "Mary, Mary" and "My Fair Lady." I rode the Greyhound bus all the way home. It took three days and is something I'll never try again due to its exhausting nature!

The summer of 1962 was a summer of firsts for me: first time in the Western United States, first time doing my own laundry, first mustache and beard, and first time traveling alone. This experience instilled in me a love of travel and photography, a love of nature, of adventure, and of learning about all things geologic. When I travel now, I rarely miss our national parks and national monuments, because it is in these places that I can reacquaint myself with nature and history and enjoy the outdoors like I did during that life-changing summer at the IU Geologic Field Station.

FEMINISM

I was born in the mid-1940s. My parents' marriage was traditional. My father worked and my mother was a homemaker. Though my parents had a traditional marriage, my father treated my mother with respect and their decisions about money, child-rearing, leisure time, etc. were made jointly. I think that their example plus my upbringing in a liberal Presbyterian church inculcated me with a sense of fairness.

My first high school job was working in a hospital pathology lab where all of the lab technicians except one were female. Meeting other women who worked outside the home was a new experience for me since none of my childhood friend's mothers worked outside the home. I very much enjoyed my time with these women and they taught me a lot about laboratory procedures and life in general. They were fun to be around.

I would be remiss if I did not mention my teachers in grade school, junior high, and high school. Most were women and they set a fine example of women in the working world. Unfortunately, at that time, most women who worked were nurses, teachers and domestics. Women in other professions were a rarity.

My wife would say that a dark chapter in my life was when I went to Wabash College, an all-male educational bastion in Crawfordsville, Indiana. There were no female professors there, but I'm happy to say that has all changed in the last 25 years. Wabash now has many superb female professors, but they have a long way to go in educating the male students and a few male professors how to treat them with respect. It was not much better in medical school. When I attended in the late 1960s I had no female professors and there were many crude jokes about women. Only about 5% of my class was women and, although they complained about mistreatment, it got them nowhere. One classmate had to plant herself on the steps of the hospital when it was time for her to deliver her first child because she had been told that the university would not deliver her, although the student health service, under their umbrella, gave her pre-partum care. One might say that these negative experiences taught me how not to treat women.

Following medical school I was fortunate to enroll in a residency in general psychiatry where there were many strong female leaders. These included the head of a state hospital female inpatient service, a hospital superintendent, a residency training director, a child psychiatric researcher, and the head of psychiatric education for medical students. I would typify them all as strong feminists. To be sure, I met with a number of male professors who were misogynists. If I were not a feminist I would certainly not be married to my wife. Her story of growing up in a conservative protestant denomination where women were subservient to men and where her mother made a pittance as a kindergarten teacher in their church-run school was shocking to me. She helped me grow as a feminist. When she was in seminary in the mid-1980s feminism, at least at some seminaries, was awakening. I read some of her seminary books as well as a number of books written by feminist Christians. The stories of these brave women made a strong impression on me. Liz's example of serving in a church with a feminist male pastor and associate female pastors has strengthened my Christianity. Her struggle to serve has strengthened my own feminism.

AFTERWORD

I hope that you have enjoyed this relatively short memoir. I'm looking forward to experiencing the next thirty or forty years of memorable events, should I live to be past 100 years of age. One can only hope!

Like the "Coming Attractions" segment at the movie theater, life is an adventure with something to breathlessly anticipate. And like a winding and sinuous highway, life is also filled with many surprises and twists and turns. There are also the dreaded potholes and irksome detours.

I can hardly wait for the next episode to begin. Maybe the next episode will begin today with my 50th high school reunion. Who knows?

Indianapolis, Indiana
October 31, 2013

SELECTED BIBLIOGRAPHY

Angelou, Maya. (1969). *I know why the caged bird sings*. New York, New York: random House.

Arana, Marie. (2001). *American Chica: Two worlds, one childhood*. New York, New York: Dell Publishing.

Barnes, Kim (1996). *In the wilderness: Coming of age in unknown country*. New York, New York: Doubleday.

Barrington, Judith (2000). *Lifesaving*. Portland, Oregon: Eighth Mountain Press.

Barry, Dan (2004). *Pull me up: A memoir*. New York, New York: W.W. Norton.

Castro, Joy (2005). *The truth book: Escaping a childhood of abuse among Jehovah's Witnesses*. Arcade Publishing.

Grogan, John (2008). *The longest trip home: A memoir*. New York, New York: William Morrow.

Hampl, Patricia (2007). *The Florist's daughter*. New York, New York: Houghton Mifflin Harcourt.

Hogan, Lisa (2001). *The woman who watches over the world*. New York, New York: W.W. Norton.

Kalish, Mildred A. (2007). *Little heathens*. New York, New York: Bantam Dell.

Karr, Mary (2000). *Cherry*. New York, New York: Viking Penguin.

Karr, Mary (1995). *The liars' club*. Viking Penguin.

Karr, Mary (2009). *Lit*. New York, New York: Harper Collins.

Lamont, Anne (1999). *Traveling mercies: Some thoughts on faith*. New York, New York: Pantheon Books.

Peterson, Eugene H. (2011). *The pastor: A memoir.* New York, New York: Harper Collins.

Steinke, Darcy (2007). *Easter Everywhere.* New York, New York: Bloomsbury.

Sterne, Arthur L. (2009). *Things I know or think I know or thought I knew or who knows?* Bloomington, Indiana: iUniverse.

Walls, Jeanette (2009). *The glass castle.* New York, New York: Scribner.

Wolff, Tobias (1989). *This boy's life: A memoir.* New York, New York: Grove Press.